Gold Coast

0.1 Gold Coast from the Sea World
helicopter, 2008.

Gold Coast
City and Architecture

Andrew Leach

LUND
HUMPHRIES

First published in 2018 by Lund Humphries

Lund Humphries
Office 3, Book House
261A City Road
London EC1V 1JX
UK

www.lundhumphries.com

ISBN: 978-1-84822-229-8

A Cataloguing-in-Publication record for this book is
available from the British Library

Copy edited by Pamela Bertram
Designed by Mark Thomson
Set in Arnhem Pro and Founders Grotesk Text
Printed in China

And what are cities really, besides signs and arbitrary boundaries?
Paul Beatty, *The Sellout* (2016)

When it comes to arts and culture, we mean business!
Cr. Tom Tate, Mayor of the Gold Coast (2012)

Contents

Acknowledgments

This book has been prepared and realised with the support of the resources and staff of the Gold Coast Libraries Local Studies Collection (Southport) and Helensvale Branch Library; Griffith University, especially members of the Gold Coast Advisory Council, Griffith School of Environment, Urban Research Program (now the Cities Research Institute), and LiveWorm; and the Gold Coast Art Gallery; the Fryer Library at the University of Queensland; the Gold Coast and Northern Rivers Region of the Australian Institute of Architects; and of my colleagues at the University of Sydney School of Architecture, Design and Planning.

Several passages in the pages that follow have been trialled in various talks, conference papers, journal articles and edited collections over the last five years: 'Neither Here Nor Elsewhere' (with Alexandra Brown), in *Anna Carey* (West End, Queensland: Queensland Centre for Photography, 2012); 'After Austerica', *Proceedings of the Society of Architectural Historians, Australia and New Zealand* (*SAHANZ*) 29, 'Fabulation: Myth, Nature, Heritage', ed. Stuart King and Steven Loo (Launceston, Tasmania: SAHANZ, 2012), 535–544; 'In Your Face, Place', *Architecture Australia* (July–August 2012): 77–80; 'The Gold Coast Moment', *Architectural Histories* 3, no. 1 (2014): 1–8; 'Lettre de la Gold Coast', *Criticat* 14 (2014): 116–124, appearing in English as 'Letter from the Gold Coast', *AA Files* 70 (2015): 24–31; 'Beyond Starlight' (with Alexandra Brown), *Proceedings of SAHANZ* 31, 'Translation', ed. Christoph Schnoor (Auckland: SAHANZ, 2014), 27–37; *GC30+: Documenting the Gold Coast Architecture Awards* (with Katherine Rickard and Finn Jones) (Southport, Queensland: Urban Research Program, Griffith University, 2015); 'Leaving Las Vegas, Again', *Grey Room* 61 (2015): 6–33; and in three chapters in *Off the Plan: The Urbanisation of the Gold Coast* (Clayton South, Victoria: CSIRO Publishing, 2016).

Research for this book was primarily supported by the Australian Research Council by way of a Future Fellowship (FT120100883). Additional project funding from Griffith University extended this support between 2012 and 2016; as did, in 2016 and 2017, the resources of the University of Sydney.

Risking the sin of omission, I want to specifically thank Michael Aird, Caryl Bosman, Ross Brewin, Alexandra Brown, Paul Burton, Maarten Delbeke, Graham Dillon, Philip Follent, Philip Goad, John Gollings, John Harwood, Bill Heather, Gordon Holden, Georgina Kreutzer, Maree Lauder, Cameron Logan, Silvia Micheli, Malcolm Middleton, Michael Mossman, Antony Moulis, Tim O'Rourke, Katherine Rickard, Robert Riddel, Ari Seligman, Hilar Stadler, Martino Stierli, Tony Styant-Browne, Nicole Sully, Wouter Van Acker and (especially) Andrew Wilson for their comments and advice along the way. The two books on the topic by Michael Jones – *A Sunny Place for Shady People* (1986) and *Country of Five*

Rivers (1988) – have offered particularly invaluable insights and syntheses of research both published and otherwise, as have the various books and articles by Robert Longhurst detailed in Further Reading at the end of this book.

At Lund Humphries, Valerie Rose has exercised patience and enthusiasm as needs have required, and together with the production team there have made publication of this work a pleasure. My thanks, in particular, to James Piper and Pamela Bertram for their efforts in shepherding the book to press.

Finally, thanks are due to Ruth and Amelia, who have since our first forays to the Gold Coast offered clear insights on the city and valuable reactions to my own, and have in many varied by vital ways propelled this book towards its inevitably sudden conclusion.

Preface

This is a book about the Gold Coast: a city and a region that nonchalantly blurs the lines between one thing and another, a situation as much maligned as emulated by Australia's state capitals, an enduring source of amusement and a setting for amusements of all kinds. Socially conservative, economically liberal, it is a city full of family parks and sportsgrounds and the culs-de-sac of suburban estates both shaped by strong visions and responding to the enduring demand for low density housing. Its cross-section from the hilly hinterland to the sea gives way suddenly to the high rises of the developers' glitter strip in Surfers Paradise. It is a dream, an escape, and a hard reality all at once. It is a city that embodies the kinds of paradoxes that arise when an experiment (in building for leisure; in free-market development) is allowed to play itself out.

This book is intended both as a foil to the popular image of the Gold Coast as being without history or substance and also as an effort to unpack a series of moments in its history that have had a hand in shaping the present-day city. It does not offer a catalogue of every architect, architectural work or bulldozed monument, but rather sets out to explain what is seen as you circle in from the north to land at Coolangatta, or as you drive towards the high-rise centre along the Gold Coast Highway towards Southport, Broadbeach or Surfers. It goes beyond the assessments that have been made of the city to date – most of which are listed as Further Reading – to ask, specifically, about the stakes of architecture in the city, not as a heritage (lost or endangered through renewal) but as a practice that simultaneously invokes the authority of the city while purporting to advance it. Within celebrations of the Gold Coast, lurks a vague and often idealised sense of the city as it once was, an authentic Gold Coast, the values of which can be recovered and expressed and that requires adherence to fixed terms of self-reflection. This tends to favour the most heroic moments of a development culture in its infancy, seemingly unfettered by rules or judgment, while at the same time bemoaning the consequences of those same forces being allowed to continue shaping the city. The Gold Coast appears different to every other Australian city, but for reasons that are common to all forms of urbanism across the country. Others have made this observation, but not for some time. To the extent that the Gold Coast is as much typical as it is exceptional, the study of the Gold Coast through its history suggests the terms for reflecting on architecture's purchase on the Australian city writ large, indeed on any city that rests as solidly as does the Gold Coast on real estate development and investment and the regulation of lifestyle as a commodity and public good.

The territory now known as 'Gold Coast' has been given a variety of names (formal and informal) throughout the last century and a half, and governed by a number of local bodies. I have used Gold Coast, therefore, as a form of shorthand as much as anything. No part of its territory was known as (the) Gold Coast before the end of the 1950s. Similarly, the territory now encompassed by the Gold Coast contained very little until the middle of the twentieth century, when it experienced its first widespread real estate boom. Some anachronisms will creep in, but I have sought to bracket these as diligently as possible.

Intentionally concise, *Gold Coast* inevitably synthesises the research of others, and this is tracked in notes and advice for 'further reading'. I have written it in situ – and for some time while teaching local architecture students about their own surroundings in a course on the architectural history of Australia. This work follows two other volumes, noted above, that approach this subject from two different perspectives: *Off the Plan* investigates the forces of urbanism from the end of the nineteenth century to the start of the twenty-first; while *GC30+* studies the professional efforts of architects in the era of the most intense architectural activity within the city, over the last three decades or so. What follows is an effort to better locate one project in the other, to identify architecture's stakes in those urbanising processes that shape the city as a whole while resisting reading those process as a consequence of architectural intentions. These pages therefore seek to trade the Gold Coast's shiny surface for texture and depth; and cliché for a slower consideration of their subject. They set out to name a local set of problems given local specificity and consider their broader import, even as they offer a primer for those encountering the Gold Coast – its towers, its beaches, its suburbs, its hinterland – for the first time.

1.1 Café Cathay at Night,
Surfers Paradise, *c.*1960.

1   To the Gold Coast!

The Victorian architect and critic Robin Boyd captured an enduring image of Queensland's Gold Coast in the portrayal he offers in *The Australian Ugliness* (1960) of its most urbanised moment – then, as now, Surfers Paradise. An ocean-side hub of apartments, hotels, restaurants and bars, Surfers is the Gold Coast's centre-by-proxy, its most visible concentration along a long ocean edge that runs from the southern end of Moreton Bay to the border towns of Coolangatta and Tweed Heads. For Boyd, writing at the end of the 1950s, Surfers Paradise embodied an over-exuberant case of the troubling tendency among Australian cities towards 'featurism', where 'building disappears beneath the combined burden of a thousand ornamental alphabets, coloured drawings and cut-outs.'[1] Although still low-rise and low density compared to the Gold Coast as it currently stands, Surfers Paradise was buried under an impenetrable layer of signs – which were, perhaps, its sum total. That is to say, in 1960 it was a city no longer shaped by those buildings to which Australians had long turned for a sense of civic gravity (the post office, banks, town halls, and public parks) so much as a city picked out in pink and orange lights.

Writing at the same moment as Boyd, the editors of the journal *Architecture in Australia* – the official mouthpiece of what was then the Royal Australian Institute of Architects (RAIA) – reflected on what they called 'the wild jungle of

1.2 Kinkabool Apartment Building and the Tahitian Sun Private Hotel, Hanlan Street, Surfers Paradise, 1960s.

indecorum' that would greet those seeking respite from the cool south. 'For a holiday', wrote the editors, 'the respectable family from the south is happy to leave drab and cold orderliness behind; for a holiday the visiting business man is eager to explore the tight alleys and dim restaurants; for a holiday mothers are pleased to loosen the carefully built and maintained family ties and children seize the opportunity of casting tighter controls off; for a holiday business girls at their prettiest and young men at their keenest find the wilderness of flickering neon signs, the throng, the perpetual crowds, the climate dictated exposure, the ceaseless offerings and lures of every kind [of] synonym to their own desire for the satisfaction denied them in their distant, orderly and boring suburban surroundings.' Positioning the 'problem' of the Gold Coast as the search for permanence within perpetual transience, they assert: 'For a holiday. But nobody would want to live with it.'[2]

In the idiosyncrasies of featurism's most extreme cases, Boyd found symptoms of widespread tendencies towards the brash and the vulgar in

Australian architecture as a mirror of Australian society. The deliberate embrace of an 'American' townscape that began, he wrote, 'in the fashionable centres of Sydney, Surfers and St Kilda Road, now oozes out evenly, flatly, to the farthest places where Australians live.'[3] This is the cultural phenomenon Boyd calls Austerica – not a land of asceticism, but of visual and material over-abundance, an (idyllic) Australia rendered (crassly) American. Boyd's account of the Gold Coast – and of Surfers Paradise especially – is humorous and penetrating. He knew the city well, before it had even been declared a city, and had settled on the terms of his judgment in the pages of *The Age* over the second half of the 1950s as the Gold Coast experimented, with the directions of its own future. The image of Surfers as a 'fibro-cement paradise under a rainbow of plastic paint' is nothing if not evocative – even if it is now regularly invoked by those nostalgic for this supposedly more straightforward past.

Australia's ugliness may be skin deep, as Boyd observes at the outset of his book, but Surfers is all skin. Despite the city's deep history,

1.3 Jeff Carter, Woman by the swimming pool with car and El Dorado Motel office behind her, Surfers Paradise, 1950s.

1.4 Jeff Carter, The Age of Ignorance, Gold Coast, 1950s.

rarely acknowledged until more recently, as an 'experience' bound up in the economic and social recovery from the Second World War it took on a specific role in Australia's cultural imagination. As Boyd goes on to note, recalling the lights and the sand, improbable fashion and 'chocolate brown' limbs: 'You might call Surfers a sort of cream, or thick skin, skimmed off the top of Australia's mid-century boom. It is rowdy, good-natured, flamboyant, crime-free, healthy, and frankly and happily Austerican.'[4]

Much has changed in the sixty years since Boyd first sketched this portrait of Surfers Paradise, which had, just a few years earlier, been a town named innocuously as South Coast. Its population, for one thing, has grown exponentially, eclipsing the pace thought extraordinary by those who had seen the numbers increase from 6,000 in 1933 to

1.5 Jeff Carter, Tents on the Beach, Gold Coast, 1950s.

1.6 Jeff Carter, The Gold Coast Real Estate
front window, Surfers Paradise, 1950s.

more than 30,000 in 1961. Now edging towards
600,000, the city has moved from being an outlier
among Australian cities to figuring as the most
populous city beyond the state capitals – even
outnumbering Canberra and Hobart to rank sixth
among the country's urban zones and the second
largest of Australia's municipalities.

Just as the series of towns and settlements that
in the wake of the Second World War formed the
adjoining towns of South Coast and neighbouring
Albert Shire in 1949, the name Gold Coast today
identifies something more akin to a cross-border
spraw (even the time-zones change in summer as
you walk across the main street that divides the

1.7 View of Surfers Paradise from
Aquarius, 2014.

'twin towns' of Coolangatta and Tweed Heads) that
now forms part of what historian Peter Spearritt has
called 'the 200 kilometre city'. The state line and
distinctions between one city and another blur as
one travels through each in the journey from the
southern border to Noosa Heads, well north of the
state capital of Brisbane, through the sprawling
conurbation of three million people that occupies
the southeast corner of Queensland.[5] Evolving road,
rail and air infrastructure has altered the Gold
Coast's relationship with Brisbane to the north
and the major cities of Sydney and Melbourne to
the south, not to mention its relationships with
Kuala Lumpur, Tokyo, Guangzhou, Dubai and
Christchurch; or with those inland mining sites
of western Queensland and the Red Centre that
underpinned its most recent property boom.[6]

As an urban form, the city of Gold Coast is
today slung between the Pacific coast and its
nearby hinterland, its cross-section offering a slow
suburban burn from the west, spiking dramatically
as it meets the water. The suburbs are populated
with unremarkable hip-roofed, off-the-plan houses,
occupying mean lots that nonetheless guarantee
each abode a lawn and a driveway. Nestled among
the snaking street circuits and culs-de-sac, gated
communities and residential retirement complexes
replicate the suburbs in miniature. The multi-lane
motorway that has grown out of successive phases
of rerouting and expansion since the 1970s – when
it replaced the Gold Coast Highway as the main
north-south road – runs a thread through the
western expanse of this sprawl, variously flanked
by housing developments, theme parks and light

1.8 View from Surfers Paradise to Burleigh
Heads, from Aquarius, 2014.

industry as it connects a series of expanding towns and cities. In contrast, all along its opposing eastern coast, houses give way to towers, with none so tall as those in Surfers Paradise and Broadbeach. Inland, navigational software struggles to keep up with the new streets being laid out west of the nineteenth-century agricultural settlement of Nerang or east of the farmland-turned-suburbia of Coomera to the city's north. Before the advent of the highly layered neo-liberal planning environment of the twenty-first century, this was for a long time a developer's playground – a light regulatory touch ensured that here, as at Surfers Paradise, matters such as public space, infrastructure and, indeed, quality in design were kept in the background.

Though the at times frenetic pace of the city's growth may be representative of the region as a whole (or, indeed, of the Australian city), the Gold Coast did not follow the typical Australian urban pattern of extending a nineteenth-century core by plan or circumstance, nor the example set by Canberra of a clear initial figure obscured over time. The retroactive establishment of a town, and then a city, by coalescing what had been independently established settlements both along the coast and inland, firmed up as a linear development that is ultimately a residue of sustained infill along the sea edge across the 1970s and 1980s. The undeveloped land of the greater Gold Coast (formed by the amalgamation of the original city of that name with Albert Shire) was turned over to housing or industry according to demand, covering over all of its previous layers of use as it reached what was, for this city, its natural endpoint. The new subdivisions realised either side of the spine formed by the motorway and intercity rail corridor read as greenfield settlements on what happen to be some of the oldest territorial claims on the city. The focus of the Gold Coast and its image is the beach and the peculiar form of development that has occurred along its edge there over the last century.

At the northern end of the high-density 50-kilometre coastal stretch are a series of settlements both historical (relatively speaking) and novel (likewise) – reaching up past Runaway Bay to Hope Island. While very different in character, each to the next, the newest of these developments follow something of the economic logic of the Gold Coast's first seaside settlement. Southport was, for example, first surveyed in 1874 and served as a setting for transporting goods from inland farms and forests to commercial ports to the north and south *and* for accommodating from the 1880s the relatively new demand for recreational sea bathing. A real estate boom of sorts followed the decision by the Governor of Queensland, Anthony Musgrave to establish his summer home there (Biddle House) on the site of what has been The Southport School since 1901, even if he and his wife were one of a large number of establishment figures who enjoyed regular visits to the seaside. Many of the oldest Southport properties either replicated the site values of the Musgrave residence elsewhere in Southport or sought prosperity through proximity. But Musgrave's preference for summer at Southport followed a tendency among holiday makers from Brisbane and the agricultural planes of the hinterland and, further away, the Darling Downs, that was well defined by the 1880s. While more difficult to reach from Brisbane, at the southern end of today's Gold Coast, Coolangatta was surveyed in 1883, when Southport was already showing promise. This border town was carved into neat beach-side subdivisions over the ensuing decades. But as the region underwent rapid expansion, these two towns (Southport being founded as such in 1918) were caught up in the merger that established the town of South Coast, which a decade later became the City of Gold Coast.

1.9 Lennon's Broadbeach Hotel, poolside with seal fountain, Broadbeach, *c.*1956.

The city earned its charter in 1959 in the era in that drew Boyd and his criticism north, and the year, too, in which Queensland marked the centenary since its foundation as a British colony. In conventional terms, the city's architectural stripes had been earned by the realisation of a series of respectable modernist buildings and developments, all offering evidence of its thriving tourism industry: in the 1950s Alfred Grant returned from travels to Florida with dreams of extensive canal estates that were planned out and implemented with the expertise of architect Karl Langer – hence Rio Vista and Miami Keys. This was translated into a city image by entrepreneur (and later mayor) Bruce Small, whose Paradise City project (again planned out by Langer) encapsulated the dream of an Australian good life. The Langer-designed 'luxury' Lennon's Hotel in Broadbeach was likewise opened for Christmas in 1956, but would in 1987 experience the sting of obsolescence after enduring a long decline – while central to the present-day Gold Coast, the Broadbeach strip was simply too isolated across the 1960s and 1970s to draw the custom envisaged at the time of its celebrated opening. The ten-storey Kinkabool was built in 1959 in Surfers Paradise (on the site of the Flamingo nightclub) to the design of the Brisbane

1.10 View towards Surfers Paradise from the RACV
Royal Pines Resort, Benowa, 2013.

practice of Ford, Hutton and Newell as the new city's first 'high-rise' hotel (quickly acquired by developer Stanley Korman); and the first stage of Korman's ambitious Chevron Hotel (designed by David Bell, from Brisbane) was furthermore opened in 1958 as a resort complex boasting facilities well beyond the basics of a room and a restaurant. In many respects, these building projects were read, and continue to be read, as coming-of-age moments that shape the reception of Gold Coast architecture as it was inaugurated in those years and codified by Boyd's criticism: a beach-side tourism city, unparalleled as it then was within Australia, if not in Hawaii or Florida, distinguished for its embrace of kitsch and its ambivalence towards the idea of 'good architecture'. The Gold Coast cemented its image among those looking its way as a place in which to play and play up; a centreless, formless city in which, for better or for worse, anyone could build and anything could get built.

In embracing the Gold Coast moniker, this town's 'founding fathers' had harnessed the power of the images conjured up by a name as the town became a city. And in the last six decades, the Gold Coast itself has changed dramatically – partly along lines laid out clearly and early on in its life as a city; and in part in ways that could not have been predicted at the moment in which the Gold Coast became the Gold Coast. Even so, Boyd's descriptions of Surfers Paradise remain fixed within a popular characterisation that the Gold Coast even now openly cultivates for itself: a criticism absorbed and then cultivated by the city and now folded into its media persona, its events calendar and the image

1.11 Property developer Eddie Kornhauser with a model of the Paradise Centre, Surfers Paradise, c.1970 (architects Hamilton Hayes Henderson).

– and for how the kind of urbanisation experienced by the Gold Coast might foreshadow that of the Australian city in general. A generation later, though, the problem had, for architectural criticism, shifted from one of possibilities and warnings to problems and consequences. After a period of intense tower construction and suburban estate development across the 1960s and 1970s and accompanied by a sustained campaign of advertorials, new home raffles and other gauche promotions in which house and lifestyle were couched as one and the same thing, the city had settled into the shape and tone it would maintain for some time. This remains the case, even as its sprawl extended further and its tallest towers became taller still. Despite the change to which it has been subject, the urbanised Pacific edge of 2018 is recognisable in the promise of the city as it stood in the mid-1980s and in the moment, therefore, in which the city's architecture profession set out to take stock of its best work, on its own (ever changing) terms. In 1959, the editors of *Architecture in Australia* – a circle in which Boyd was no stranger – posed a question that still seemed open into the 1980s: 'Why have civic fathers with wide vision, townplanners and architects with authority and talent stayed so shyly in the background?'[7]

Arguing an enduring and collective lapse of judgment on the part of the Gold Coast's architects

of the city-spectacle. The beachfront skyline of 2018 – with the promise of a tower to overshadow even the spire of Q1 (a phrase that may well seem quaint to future readers, given the city's history) – would have been unrecognisable to Boyd. Likewise, the winding, low-density suburbs that have crept their way west towards the hinterland, and north towards the Logan River. Or the M1 and Gold Coast-to-Brisbane Airport rail lines servicing Australia's most intense corridor of commuter traffic. The modest homes that once lined the canals of the Nerang River have been swapped out in patterns that give a snap insight into the long-term performance of the property market across the city. And the ocean edge has been a palimpsest as casual shacks have given way to established houses, demolished in turn for two, or three, generations of apartment towers of increasing ambition.

In many respects, Boyd's concern was for what the city was about to become, given the evidence

1.12 View of proposed skyscraper apartment building, Burleigh Heads, September 1971 (architects Merrin and Cranston).

1.13 Daw's Paradise Driveway Shell Service
Station, Surfers Paradise, 1959 (designed by
Geoffrey Styant-Browne).

and town planners, Sydneysider Neville Gruzman
followed in Boyd's footsteps to dismiss any efforts to
gauge the role of those professions in a city that had
been, and continued to be, live with opportunities
for build – even if, as local designers themselves
would freely admit, the work they made could vary
in its quality. Supported by a robust local media,
the Gold Coast Division of the RAIA staged its first
annual architecture awards in 1984 – a chapter to
which we will return, but which prompted a fresh
discussion on the nature of the commissions
acquired by architects on the Gold Coast, and of
the limitations and opportunities introduced by the
idiosyncratically instrumental role for architecture
as a profession in the service of property
development. And so, speaking for cultured souls
across the country, sensitive to Boyd's prescience,
Gruzman responded with commentary targeting the
deplorable consequences of a sustained period of
famously unguided development along the sea edge,
asserting that 'it is a disaster which should be bulldozed into the surf.'[8]

For Boyd, first reporting on the Gold Coast from
his 1957 summer vacation, it was the displacement
of the building by the sign and all that it presaged
as the Australian city descended into a cultureless
hell of its own making. (Indeed, responding to his
own holiday impressions, J. B. Priestley in 1961
recalled the exclamation of a fictional local named
Rosaria, though for the city's supplanting of nature
rather than its negation of culture: 'I hate those
places so much I wish a great wave would come one
night and push them into the sea.'[9]) Today, fresh
problems are posed by the apparent neutrality of
architectural work in a city in which architectural
ideas play second fiddle to its operation and
expansion. Allowing for a little fine grain, these
positions on the Gold Coast remain very much in
play, as of course they do less overtly in all cities.
For many the high-rise path from Southport
to Broadbeach will remain an eyesore, an
abomination, and an object lesson in the need for
controls over real estate development and public
space. The pop culture response has, naturally,

been to embrace the trash from the safe distance of criticism, or to invoke something deeper, detached from the settings of *Gold Coast Cops* and *Muriel's Wedding*. Learning, yet again. But these kinds of safe resistance have been folded into the image the city has sought to project: an edgy persona tempered by the amenities of a controlled urban design balancing the needs of the rate-paying base, the steady tourist flow and the economic injections of the major event, fashioning 'lifestyle' from the raw materials of development.

In the face of a certain resistance to probe beneath the city's skin, this book poses two questions. What happened on the Gold Coast to make it the Gold Coast? And why should we care? To put it another way, when we cast an eye over its shorefront skyline or across its seemingly endless, anonymous suburbs, what exactly can we see? And what has been covered over in the process of its realisation? Whether you ponder these questions having come to the city for the briefest of stays, or having been happily soaking in it for decades, there is a depth to the city beyond its local lore and colourful characters that is, to put it simply, *important* as a chapter in Australian urbanism. Important for getting beyond a simplification of the city as a product of free-wheeling development or of the advent of the motorcar or of the present-day city as an extension of the sleepy settlements that preceded it – although these factors play their part in its history. Some readers will not easily recognise Boyd's characterisation of an intense urbanity, keeping an eye on Surfers Paradise from the middle distance of suburban surrounds from which they rarely stray. Some will be fighting for change: greater intensity on one side, and ever more development; protected pockets of environmental, architectural and urban heritage on the other, resisting the forces that have shaped the city up to now. Others still will wrestle with legacies of crime and corruption that both frame the city and tarnish (or perhaps even consolidate) its image.

In the immediate wake of the 1994 amalgamation of the City of Gold Coast with neighbouring Albert Shire, extending the city to the west and to the north, something shifted in the Gold Coast's relationship with its own image. This responded, in part, to the kind of sentiments to which Gruzman had given voice in 1984 and which were recalled regularly by those who sensed they had something to defend. It did not exactly jettison the values to which Boyd gave expression in *The Australian Ugliness*. Instead, it turned them over from criticism to nostalgia, reframing a distinct lack of planning as layers of planning – a gesture given most obvious expression in the planning document *Gold Coast Urban and Heritage Character Study*, which was published in 1997 and to which we will return in a later chapter. The city remains in the moment that is captured by that study and into which it had entered in the middle of the 1990s, not so much a matter of existential reflection (what *is* the Gold Coast?!) as an awkward preoccupation with what has proven to be a set of self-sustaining clichés. Part of the urban (and architectural) history of the Gold Coast, then, is also the history of the image of the city, both formed from afar and held close.

The pages that follow pose the question of what the Gold Coast has been at a series of crucial moments – or timespans – in the history of a region rendered into a territory and, eventually, into a city. There is much that is particular about the history of the Gold Coast, as we will see, but also much that is common with the experience of those cities in Australia, Asia, the Pacific and elsewhere that have altered dramatically through their encounter with the forces and events of the nineteenth and twentieth centuries. Among the first myths to dispel are the Gold Coast's novelty, the absence of its history – its cultural superficiality. And to these that we next turn.

2.1 Kombumerri Park, Merrimac, 2017.

2   Under the Surface

The most famous mode of modern development on the Gold Coast is undoubtedly the canal estate, effected in various projects dating from the second half of the 1950s and even now continuing to shape new real estate ventures. Making an initial claim on the Nerang River, the names of these estates evoke the distant model of a modern American opulence: Rio Vista, Paradise City, Florida Gardens, et cetera, around which formed part of Boyd's impressions of Austerica, gathering as the thick cream on the surface of Australia's post-war prosperity. The planning of their streets, provision of amenities and sale of their image all relied upon an informal approach to development on the part of the both the South Coast and Albert Shire. These projects largely evaded, through their novelty, an otherwise unsuspecting pair of governing urban bodies and a state legislature that had not predicted the kind of relationship with the Nerang and other waterways that developers were only too eager to exploit. These projects relied, too, upon the force of will propelled by the values these estates advanced, with their images of progress, comfort, and a sense of having arrived. Drained in the first decades of the twentieth century, this area had long been dismissed by surveyors and nineteenth-century settlers alike as the Great Swamp. But its time had come.

While the Gold Coast's story of settlement and progress favours those who arrived and made something of the land and its resources – from timber to sun and sand – the land had been occupied for centuries, millennia even. This history is barely known, if at all, by today's Gold Coasters. A few place names and the bare bones of an urban pre-history hardly register against the noise of the post-war boom and the test it seems to offer of a local authenticity. Against the impression of the Gold Coast as something made from nothing, however, is a multilayered narrative of occupation and economy on which the successive development booms of the twentieth and twenty-first centuries would blithely build.[1]

Among the moments when the region's indigenous history has intersected or been overlaid by the post-settlement, urban history of the Gold Coast, the discovery of the burial ground near what is now called Kombumerri Park (fig. 2.1) is one of the most significant. It defines and embodies two distinct scales for the region's past. One belongs to a deep history spanning tens of thousands of years and made difficult, today, by the colonial experience cast by some as an invasion and others as progressive settlement – which read either way changed irrevocably the traditional relationship between the region's people and the country on which they had long lived. The other is of a comparatively superficial history of the city as an experiment in free-market development, building on a colonial-era approach to 'discovery', cultivation and enterprise. It is inevitable, though, that when people have lived and died in a region for millennia, as they have on what we now know as the Gold Coast, the buried traces of that past will from time to time rise to the surface. Sometimes culture and history are forced to give way to progress (as it were), acknowledging the facts of the past and their significance while pouring the footings of future development.

For the most part, the modern and contemporary encounter with this thick stratum of the city's history has been at a small scale and treated as a mild inconvenience to be quickly put beyond sight. In some cases, it has been openly acknowledged as part of the region's heritage, as in the case of the siting of the Gold Coast Historical Society on a site in Elliot Street (Surfers Paradise) that had served, variously, as a midden and burial ground up to the end of the nineteenth century. In the absence of formal archaeological studies of the site, no one can tell the precise age of its unearthed artefacts, but the assumption that they reflect many centuries of use is more than reasonable.[2]

Contemporary Australian society is limited in its understanding and valuing of the way that people interacted with the land before it was colonised and rendered a productive territory feeding imperial networks and modern economies. Protocols and protections have been established in recent decades for managing the archaeological finds that recall the realities of Australia's pre-European past, but they do not capture all aspects of Aboriginal culture, like language, historical ecologies, or significant landscapes. The importance since the 1980s of the term 'Kombumerri' to describe the families anchored to Southport and the southern Moreton Bay and since the 1990s of 'Yugambeh' (or, since the 1950s, 'Bunjalung') to denote a language group spanning across to Beaudesert and the Scenic Rim has followed the success of local families in asserting the enduring presence of Aboriginal families and their shared culture from the Brisbane River to the Northern Rivers of New South Wales. This, of course, notwithstanding the fluidity of boundaries between what we might be tempted to read as defined tribal areas, readily crossed by marriage and other factors.[3] And notwithstanding, too, the contemporary political agency advanced

by now widely used tribal or language labels that are not universally accepted by those people they purport to name.

In an episode in the construction of the 'Australian dream', what is now known as the Broadbeach Aboriginal Burial Ground was discovered by accident in June 1963, a result of landscaping contractors pilfering the site's rich soil for the gardens being laid down throughout the new canal estate developments extending inland into the area now called Broadbeach Waters and Merrimac. Landscapers encountered the remains of what would amount, on closer study, to more than two hundred people, first (incorrectly) treated as evidence of suspicious settler deaths (and attended by police); then as an archaeological find, catalogued, removed, processed and conserved by researchers at the University of Queensland across the mid-1960s and long held by the University's Anatomy Department in spite of objections raised by their modern custodian–descendants. The remains ranged in vintage from around AD 780 to 1860, evidencing more than a thousand years of continued use of the site for burials; and dating, too, beyond the moment in the early nineteenth century when escaped convicts sought refuge south of the Logan River and British-Australian settlers began to farm cotton and sugar and extract timber between the Logan and Tweed.

Half a century ago, while documenting and protecting the burial site, now occupied by the playing grounds of Merrimac State High School, archaeologists did not have the benefit of either established cultural protocols or legislative direction; nor did the region's Aboriginal people have the voice to ensure a culturally appropriate – or indeed ethical – treatment of their ancestors' remains. In the absence of any these protections or the resources to guard the site against further pilfering, the removal of these remains on balance likely ensured their preservation, albeit at a cultural cost. Certainly, the archaeological team, led by Laila Haglund, could claim to have saved the remains from total dispersal, and there is little to suggest that contractors would have traded good soil for cultural respect in the middle of the 1960s. The site was hardly insignificant, though, ultimately proving to be the setting of the largest burial excavation undertaken in Australia to that time. This initiated a long and exhausting battle to see these ancestral remains returned to their original resting place – a battle in which the value of the city's Aboriginal heritage to the city itself (not to mention Australia) was ultimately in question.[4]

Beyond the argument that the University offered protection was, of course, its counterpoint, namely that the first peoples of the Gold Coast had the right for their ancestors to remain undisturbed, even if it stymied the Gold Coast's development prospects. Servicing a new local population, the high school had, however, opened in 1979, more than fifteen years after the discovery of the site and several years before the question of the proper treatment of those buried at Broadbeach had been settled. This removed the possibility of reinstating the burial ground on its traditional site. Instead, the suburban park behind the school was, in 1988, dedicated to the task and the remains were interred within a subtly inflected landscape, neither overtly funerary nor memorial in its form, with a simple sign explaining the significance of the site. A planting programme was shared by modern descendants of those ancestors whose remains had been disturbed along with members of other indigenous communities from the wider region, local officials and neighbours. It returned to the park those trees and ferns that had long supported the birds that had spiritual significance to the local people, including (notes the public sign) 'the eagle, the king parrot, the land curlew, the night heron and jingree-jingree (willie wagtail).' The disturbed remains were quietly absorbed by the park, 500 metres from where they were first unearthed and under conditions recreated to reflect 'the ancient homeland as exactly as present conditions would permit.'[5]

Given the clash of tradition and progress played out in and around this site, it speaks to the interactions of the thin, if totalising, layer of post-settlement culture with that of the region's long-standing and original indigenous life – extending to more than two *hundred* centuries – which is hardly

constrained to the setting of today's Broadbeach Waters and, indeed, spreads across the substrate of the entire expanse of this modern city. As such, it is caught between erasure and recognition, tolerance and respect. On one level, this is a question of the city's immaterial heritage and of the multitude of pasts on which it can draw in cultivating its image. On another, it is a matter of how the Gold Coast, as a city that relies on the image, deals with the many conflicting layers that lend substance to that which it projects as being properly its own and against which it consequently invites assessment.[6]

This history remains difficult, though – it is confronting, contentious and hard to pin down. West of the Gold Coast, in the Scenic Rim town of Tamrookum, a memorial to the Munaljahli people of the Logan and Albert rivers, and to William and Emily Williams in particular (1847–1927 and 1856–1929, respectively), was erected in 1990. On this occasion, a Williams' descendant recalled one reality of the encounter with the region's first Anglo-Australian settlers. Of William Williams he recalled: 'He was there when the first white men came. When the police came to take the families off to the reserves, William gathered up his family and headed into the hills. Only a few of the original families remained in the area.'[7]

Early accounts of contact between British and Aboriginal people belie an uneven experience of the encounter with the colonial world. Many explorers, timber-getters and traders were welcomed, fed and protected by the communities they met, and indeed depended on them for shelter and sustenance. The timber-getter Ned Harper, for instance, who will reappear in the next chapter, had Aboriginal children, and historical accounts have local people accompanying the newcomers on their forays into the forests.[8] Accounts of basic settler houses being roofed in bark indicates a technological reliance on the region's Aboriginal people, who had developed refined and reliable techniques for living off the land. As the nineteenth century crossed its half-way mark, however, with the arrival of pastoralists and the plantation estates, the fortunes of the region's indigenous people became rather more mixed.

What was once a thriving and populous community, living on its own terms, witnessed an irreversible change to its way of life. Many Aboriginal people were indeed killed or 'dispersed' by the Queensland Native Police and by armed civilians who were not held accountable for their actions. Many, though, remained in the region, albeit on the new terms offered by the settler industries of plantation agriculture – in the case of Williams, working for the celebrated pastoralist Robert Collins (who campaigned for those forests still unspoiled by extraction to be named national parks).[9] The celebrated nineteenth-century figure known as 'Jackey Jackey King of the Logan and Pimpama' helped his extended family to work with settlers on farms and in the fields, thereby ensuring their safety, to a degree, through integration with the newcomers.[10]

Despite a record of violence towards the Aboriginal people of today's Gold Coast, there was not a systematic clearing, as such, of the land in that region. Families remained in the area, setting aside aspects of a traditional life with the land as an apparently necessary compromise in favour of the modern modes of living introduced by farmers and consolidated in the townships established across the nineteenth century. But while a connection to earlier generations had not been entirely severed by white settlement, the significant landscape of forests, swamps, rivers and beach that had long offered food and shelter had been appropriated and turned to other purposes. This forced a decisive break with the past that would occur over the course of a century or more as rivers and swamps, fishing grounds and oyster beds were turned over to private ownership or eradicated through development.

So, much is lost. Among the ways in which we can, today, figure the pre-contact occupation of the country now absorbed into the architectural and urban history of Gold Coast city-region, is to recall the observations of early, nineteenth-century visitors to the mainland or nearby Minjerribah (Stradbroke Island, split in two at Jumpinpin Channel after 1894) to build up an image of the villages that predated the arrival in great numbers of timber-getters and farmers from Brisbane and elsewhere.[11] (As a signal

of the scale of the population on the island/s, an early archaeological study by V. V. Ponosov found nearly 150 midden sites over what are now two islands.[12]) Precious little of the fabric described by these narratives remains, although they suggest stable settlements responding to the seasons and to the concomitant cycles of ecological and economic change.

The most thorough-going synthesis of these accounts is Tim O'Rourke's essay 'Aboriginal Camps and "Villages" in Southeast Queensland'. He therein characterises eighteenth and nineteenth-century descriptions of village sites as those of 'habitual campsites occupied according to seasonal, economic and socio-cultural patterns' – not permanent villages with an enduring architecture so much as sites of long-term importance for the region's original occupants.[13] Matthew Flinders had recorded his observations of Aboriginal people in Moreton Bay in 1799, to which many other accounts were added over the next half century as convicts, escapees, free settlers and colonial administrators found their way to Brisbane, and from there through the present-day Gold Coast to Port Macquarie in New South Wales. These are not interchangeable, by any means, but offer some suggestions as to how people lived in the southern part of Moreton Bay and across the rivers from the Nerang to the Tweed. The shipwrecked convicts Thomas Pamphlett (James Groom), Richard Parsons and John Finnegan in 1823 recalled to John Uniacke of John Oxley's expedition, five or so camps of similar size along the length of their temporary home on Minjerribah (where they ate well and enjoyed local hospitality). British explorers noted bora grounds and kippa-rings which had been used for ceremonies.

The security of the seasons meant that communities were less migratory than elsewhere across the continent, and 'evidence supports repeated and long-term occupation of … habitual campsites.'[14] Windbreaks and a ready supply of construction materials ensured that huts were either protected or quickly rebuilt if they needed to be. According to these early accounts, buildings themselves varied according to function and

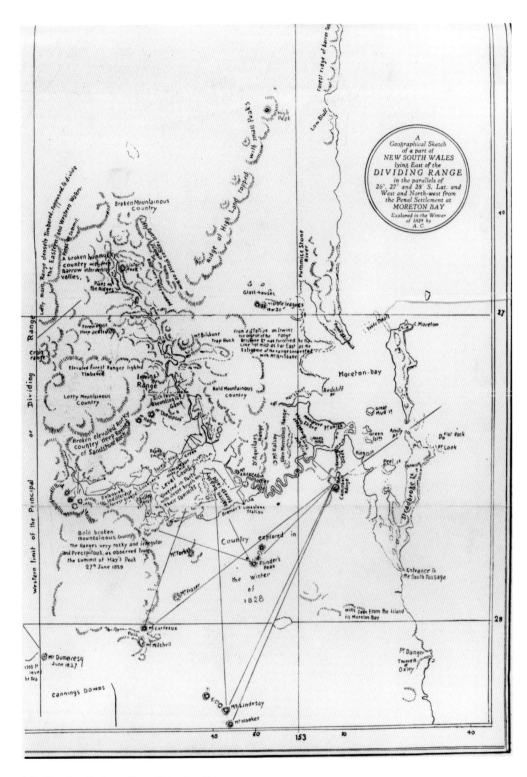

2.2 Allan Cunningham, Map of Moreton Bay district, 1829.

2.3 A dwelling on Stradbroke Island in the late 1800s.

food, and the consistency of fishing seasons – and the reliability of other food sources – meant that in recent history, at least, these camps were fairly stable. The subsistence economy followed a seasonal calendar related to annual climatic patterns and corresponding resource availability.'[15]

Regarding the appearance of these camps, Flinders recorded his observations of one to the south of Bribie Island, located north of Minjerribah: five or six huts of around four metres in length, resembling 'a covered arch-way, rounded at the far end' (compare fig. 2.3). According to a mid-nineteenth-century account by Tom Petrie of his travels in Moreton Bay, some huts he had seen were too small to allow someone to stand; others were larger and 'much wider, and held about ten people' – reflecting variations in function and status. Petrie describes a construction method whereby saplings would be bent over in situ, one end stuck into the ground to make a series of hoops that were then covered over with weaving and melaleuca bark.[16] Early images from the region either capture or approximate how they may have once appeared.

status. O'Rourke notes recurring references to camps of 'bark-clad dwellings' among the few detailed descriptions from this time (even if these descriptions are uneven in quality). 'Communities relied on the ocean and coastal waterways for

2.4 Indigenous homes near Cave Point,
Fingal Head (New South Wales), 1911.

Not with any certainty, but suggesting how houses and camps might also have looked to those timbergetters who first made their way across from the Tweed and needed shelter of their own.

If early visitors and settlers had the benefit of Aboriginal building techniques, a photograph from Cave Point on the Tweed River at Fingal Head indicates how traditional structures acquired a tentative permanence by incorporating such materials as corrugated iron into their fabric (fig. 2.4).

Roughly contemporaneous with Petrie's *Reminiscences of Early Queensland*, was James Backhouse's account of the area between Brisbane and the Tweed River, and of the islands in and around Moreton Bay, published 1843 as *A Narrative of a Visit to the Australian Colonies*. Backhouse included a woodcut image (fig. 2.5) of a rounded dwelling on Minjerribah, clad in bark over a light frame. He likened the structures in the camp he visited to the 'tilts' of an English traveller's camp, 'a number of huts, formed of arched sticks, and covered with tea-tree bark, so as to form weather-tight shelters, just high enough … to sit upright in them.'[17] He noted that the communities would move among various campsites on the island (some of which being coastal, others being on more elevated ground) depending on the weather and the availability of food. In the absence of corresponding documentation of dwellings south of the Logan River, we are left to imagine how the established camps that were described by early visitors might have appeared.

While twentieth-century histories of the Gold Coast have favoured the pioneering spirit of the first cedar-getters on the Richmond, Tweed, Nerang, Coomera and Logan rivers, the break they forced with traditional patterns of living, and traditional approaches to building and shelter, means that it required determination to picture everyday life before the British incursions into the area. This has been made more difficult through the clash of cultural values that has characterised the contemporary Gold Coast experience of artefacts and sites predating the colonial era. In 2005, curator and anthropologist

2.5 An Aboriginal hut on Stradbroke Island in 1843, woodcut based on observations by James Backhouse in *A Narrative of a Visit to the Australian Colonies* (1843), 374.

Michael Aird lamented that archaeological sites were more often than not eclipsed by 'the develop-at-all-costs mentality', which forced a trade of preservation for documentation. 'Nobody is really in a position to stop development over a few stone artefacts.'[18] Mid-nineteenth-century impressions and descriptions of indigenous communities and their environments around Moreton Bay capture a region's culture at the brink of fundamental disruptions to living patterns and habitats established over thousands of years. Evidence of this life before the British Empire made its own claim on the region has been unearthed through development of property and urban infrastructure, offering fragmented insights into the long-term use of the territory on which the Gold Coast has sat for such a comparatively short time. Those fragments more often than not show how the nineteenth-century irruption of towns built around important locations of river-side industry or at strategic moments in communication and trade between major settlements in Queensland and New South Wales, was presaged (albeit imperfectly) by a deep and knowing appreciation of the value of those sites in maintaining communities and facilitating communication and trade.

The quandary described by Aird, which was in that instance raised by the widening of the Waterford-Tamborine Road, echoes across the city

2.6 Aerial view of Surfers Paradise looking across
the Nerang River to Paradise Waters, 1982.

and over decades. Twenty years earlier, in 1986, the development of Helensvale's River Downs Estate (alongside the Saltwater Creek, which feeds into the Coomera River and Lake Coombabah in turn), earthworks uncovered more than four hundred fragments of stones and shells of archaeological significance. At that time Aird observed of the efforts in which he was involved: 'We're just trying to save these things before someone builds a house.'[19]

At the other end of the city that same year, an Aboriginal midden was likewise unearthed while workers were building a walkway linking the Tallebudgera Creek Wetlands to Fleay's Fauna Reserve in West Burleigh. Weighing up the city's priorities, Mayor Alderman Denis Pie (who chaired the Gold Coast Visitors and Convention

Bureau before taking up the mayoralty) said it was 'unfortunate' for these relics to be disturbed, but that they needed to be considered within the larger scene of the Gold Coast's reliance on income through tourism – an economy in which what is now the David Fleay Wildlife Park and the Currumbin Animal Sanctuary have long played a central role.[20] The Maybree Middens on the banks of the Tallebudgera Creek were among more than a dozen midden sites dating back up to six thousand years known to be threatened by tourism-led development.[21] A decade later, another midden described as 'a cultural antiquity', uncovered in construction of a car park in the vicinity of Coombabah, contained evidence of pathways extending back five millennia between the lake and the Coomera River.[22]

While these sites may seem slightly out of the way to visitors to today's Gold Coast, beyond the urban concentration of the beach, the Marriott Hotel is not. Sitting alongside the Nerang River at Main Beach, it occupies a site named Jarri Parila, which invokes the historical importance of that setting as a place of meeting and feasting. The river-bend retains the name Jarriparilla Cove, reflecting its longstanding importance in the region's cultural ecology and economy, but even as early as the 1980s (when the photograph of fig. 2.6 was taken) it was a setting of intensive residential development, including the Atlantis vertical community tower designed by the Heather Thiedeke Group (1982) and the first wave of high-rise buildings that swapped out the low-density occupation of Paradise Waters and Main Beach.

While these many sites offered strong evidence of the enduring importance of the Gold Coast's natural ecology for the region's indigenous Australians, their story did not yet figure in the image even recently being cultivated by the city. But they are hardly peripheral to the city as it stands. A short walk to the north of the ungainly bulk of the Gold Coast Convention Centre are the Cascade Gardens (figs 2.7–2.8), built by local Rotarians at the start of the 1950s on a river-bend of the Nerang River. Beyond a family park, picnic ground and fishing spot, it is home to the Queensland Korean War Memorial and the Kokoda Memorial Walk. Those qualities that commend the park now have, though, commended it for centuries, and a midden there quietly speaks to its long-standing importance as somewhere that sustained a community.

The anglicised approximations of names in the region's original language (called Yugambeh) that pepper the Gold Coast map – Pimpama, Coombabah, Tamborine Mountain, Nerang, Bundall, Benowa and Currumbin, to give examples – already began to cover over their original sense through the corruptions of recording in writing an oral tongue.[23] This loss is important to register given the highly descriptive nature of these place

2.7 Cascade Gardens Picnic Reserve looking to Little Tallebudgera Creek, Broadbeach, 1967.

2.8 Cascade Gardens Picnic Reserve, view
from Florida Gardens, 2017.

2.9 Jebbribillum Bora, Burleigh Heads, view
across the Gold Coast Highway, 2017.

names, which account for topographical and botanic characteristics as well as specific food sources (once) found plentifully in one place or another. It is important to note, too, as an example of the way that the Gold Coast as a modern city overwrites itself in the manner of a palimpsest. The bora ring at the northern end of Burleigh Heads (fig. 2.9), sitting alongside the four-lane Gold Coast Highway, was protected from development as early as 1913 through the intervention of local Nerang Shire councillor James Appel, but is a rare instance of a site of ceremonial or cultural importance being kept as something apart from the city – and indeed it is only one of three bora that cleared the turn of the twentieth century and survived its full duration.[24] The Gold Coast's Aboriginal culture has been reinscribed into its history in recent years, not least through the agency of such organisations as the Jellurgal Aboriginal Cultural Centre and the Yugambeh Museum, but it was long considered irrelevant to the Gold Coast as a town that was built on nothing and has made its own way at its own pace.

A visit to today's Coombabah wetlands (figs 2.10–2.12) offers a glimpse into the kind of vast landscape that once covered the area now named Helensvale, Coombabah and Biggera Waters: mangrove swamps giving way to a lake that is now the view of a privileged few and waterways feeding Moreton Bay that have been shaped to the needs of the local real estate market. But while measures of environmental protection have helped to maintain the wetlands as a conservation area, they no longer serve as they once did to bring together the region's clans. *Gold Coast Bulletin* reporter Frank Hampson exercised a tempting anachronism in his *In the Beginning was the Dreamtime*: 'Long before white settlement, tribes of Aborigines used to walk 200 kilometres to holiday on the Gold Coast, taking part in great seafood corroborees and storytelling.'[25] If this could be said of the edges of Lake Coombabah, it could be said, too, of almost all of the waterways passing through the Gold Coast: the Nerang River, Tallebudgera Creek and Coomera River have each in turn, at different moments in time and under varied rationales, been repurposed to modern needs that

have undermined their traditional functions.

The fragmented material realities recovered through archaeological documentation and analysis are fleshed out by the historical imagination that places these fragments into conversation with the pictorial and narrative accounts of life among Aboriginal people at the moment of first British contact. Those few sites that have won a place in today's popular imagination as sites of abiding spiritual significance allow us to forget that the entire landscape is inscribed with meaning. Among sites of contemporary importance, the imposing headland of the Burleigh Head National Park (gazetted in 1947, fig. 2.13) deserves particular mention for its prominence in local mythology. Overlooking the Tallebudgera Creek, the headland of Big Burleigh is held to have been formed when the spirit giant Jabreen took his rest after a day's hunting and a swim, to cool down, out to the horizon and back. Called Jellurgal after the beehive (or 'sugarbag') from which he ate honey, he went to the shore to wash his hands. On stretching up to his full height, the land rose as far as his fingertips, thus forming the headland. The hexagonal shafts of basalt (extending up to four metres in length, fig. 2.14) are his fingers, reaching out towards the ocean.[26] [...] Protected for its natural beauty rather than its cultural importance, Jellurgul (a name otherwise recorded as Challangoor, reflecting the imperfect translation of the name into written form) is within a protected area of 27 hectares – and from the air reads as an abrupt and rare curtailment of the creep of Burleigh's medium-density suburban ambitions.[27]

This, though, is a now-protected fragment of those landforms, swamps, forests and waterways with which the original Gold Coasters lived for thousands, indeed tens of thousands of years before white settlement applied an entirely new logic – territorial and economic – to the region. It is easy to rehearse those sacred sites that have risen to prominence by having one way or another been spared the developer's bulldozer, but a visit to the protected edge of Lake Coombabah offers a constrained glimpse into a world when all

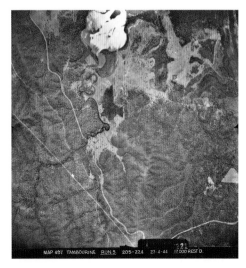

2.10 High aerial over Helensvale, Coombabah and Arundel, 1944.

2.11 Coombabah Wetlands, view of mangrove swamp, 2017.

2.12 Lake Coombabah, 2017.

2.13 Aerial view of the Burleigh headland and the mouth of
Tallebudgera Creek, taken from Palm Beach, 1978.

landscape had meaning for its role in sustaining communities physically or in embodying the host of ancestors who had once walked on the land.

In his brief but important analysis of the Gold Coast's 'First Inhabitants' for the *John Oxley Journal*, Robert Longhurst sums up the fate of this deep history in these memorably despondent lines:

> Two bora rings, a few words, bones and implements are all that today remain of what may have been one of the most concentrated Aboriginal populations ... in Australia. Europeans have, in the space of little more than a century, destroyed the swamps, altered the course of rivers, built on the dunes and wallum plains, reconstructed the beaches, and consequently eradicated the wildlife which sustained the aborigine and had spiritual significance beyond our understanding. Highways now pass over burial grounds, and the Burleigh bora-ring, where young males were once initiated into the secrets and responsibilities of adulthood, is increasingly surrounded by more motels, flats and apartment buildings. The spirit Jabreen, who in the dreamtime created Jebbribillum (Little Burleigh) and Jellurgul (Burleigh Head), is forgotten.[28]

In 1980, when Longhurst wrote this, our ability to appreciate the cultural depth of the city perhaps looked less promising than it does now. The remains from the Broadbeach Aboriginal Burial Ground had not yet been returned to the land from which they

2.14 Jabreen's 'fingers', Jellurgal, Burleigh Heads, 2017.

2.15 Aerial view of Burleigh Heads looking
towards Burleigh Head National Park, 1982.

were removed; and the move to cultivate widespread respect for Australia's indigenous cultures was still in its infancy. (Remember, too, that it had not even been two decades at this point since indigenous Australians were counted in the census, or allowed to vote in national elections, and only fifteen years since Queensland became the last state to allow Aboriginal votes in its elections.) But no history of the Gold Coast that celebrates the modernist boom of the 1950s as an exercise of exploiting virgin land and latent waterways can justifiably ignore the layers of occupation and use that have given those sites enduring significance.

In this, the introduction of the ancestral remains removed from the Broadbeach Burial Ground into the newly designated Kombumerri Park offers an analogy for the Aboriginal history of the Gold Coast region: absorbed into a new kind of landscape (and the city) as a new form of occupation; a series of subtle inflections, easily missed, but which when registered offer profound moments of pause.

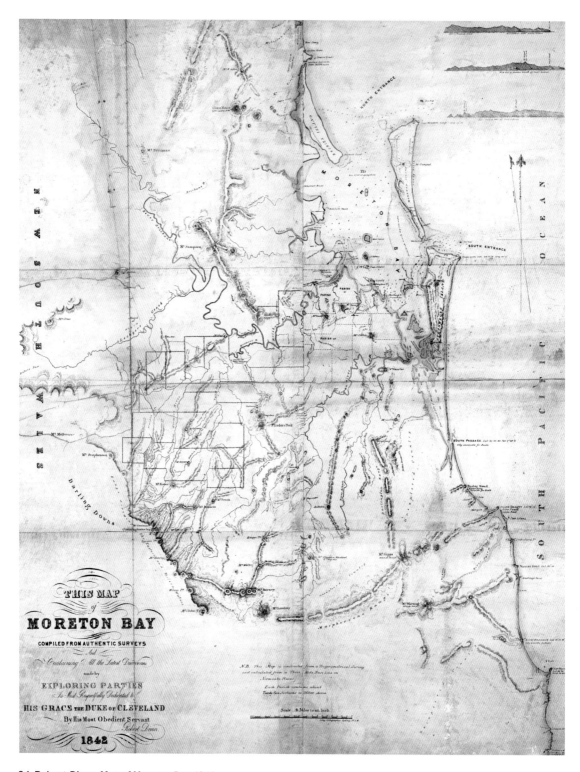

3.1 Robert Dixon, Map of Moreton Bay, 1842.

3   River Bound

In his 1971 book *Los Angeles: The Architecture of Four Ecologies*, the English architectural historian Reyner Banham observed the different outlook of the city of LA, settled from inland, where the sea is a hard limit, from that of San Francisco, settled by sea, where it serves as a beginning.[1] The Gold Coast may never have been settled by sea in the sense that Brisbane and Sydney were settled by sea, but the nineteenth-century history of the territory on which this city would be built can be described in terms of two competing attitudes declaring the beach either a hard edge or an open beginning: for the early agriculturalists and timber-getters, a limit; for the burgeoning recreational entrepreneurs, a resource in its own right.

The town incorporated in 1949 as South Coast consolidated the management of a series of seaside settlements, spanning from Southport in the north to the southern border town of Coolangatta. Southport had sought from the late 1870s to serve as a genteel seaside town in counterpoint to Brisbane, while the origins of Surfers Paradise in Elston, some decades later, offered a more open experiment in real estate development. Burleigh Heads and Coolangatta, too, were formalised around property estates, with the southern villages taking on a new importance during the Pacific War as Allied servicemen enjoyed recreational leave on their beaches. Southport and Coolangatta were early participants in the Australian network of airports (terrestrial and marine) in the 1930s and 1940s. But half a century earlier they connected, too, with Brisbane by means of a rail network that had been laid out before any of these settlements had given cause for investment in this infrastructure, moving goods and people from the end of the 1880s (and Coolangatta from 1903) to the end of the 1950s. Long before the Southport Rail Service brought from Beenleigh those who would enjoy a restorative spell recreating on the Broadwater, however, the primary goal of Queensland's transportation networks had been to move goods from a productive hinterland to the capital, and from there to various points on the map of the British Empire and its trading partners.

In this, much of the Gold Coast as it is now defined – from the border established in 1859 to the plane south of the Logan River – was not settled first at the seaside, but inland, responding to opportunities to turn an 'uncultivated' terrain to profit.

The arrival of the first British settlers to the land between the Logan and Tweed rivers followed closely on the heels of the establishment of the Moreton Bay convict settlement and penal colony, which was in operation from 1824 to 1839 in what was claimed as British territory under the governance of New South Wales. At its peak, the foreign population of Brisbane numbered no more than 1,200 in these years, making it very much a minority settlement among the established indigenous communities.

The wetlands and alluvial planes extending from the south of Brisbane to the Border Ranges (as they would come to be called) were crossed by a series of rivers and creeks – the Logan, Pimpama, Coomera, Nerang, Currumbin, Tallebudgera and Tweed – all having been in use for centuries, but which from the middle of the nineteenth century were turned over to crops, then farmed with cattle, as the timber of the hinterland forests was systematically extracted and the lands cleared for agriculture.

The Colony's Surveyor-General, John Oxley, had mapped the coastline in his efforts to locate an ideal site for a convict settlement, in the meantime documenting Moreton Bay and its islands, as well as the Pacific coast, past the present-day state border towards what is now Port Macquarie. His was not the first mission to chart this part of Australia, however, with maps having been made by vessels passing by since the sixteenth century, and with Cook's *Endeavour* having charted the coast in 1770. The area between the Logan and the Tweed, though, was not registered in any of these charts with any degree of detail, which meant that the territories inland from the charted coast were something of an open question for those who ventured south of Brisbane in the 1820s and 1830s. The first Britons to do so, and thereby shaping the region as a site of white settlement, included those who had left the prison system (some having served their time, others not), along with others who had joined the free settlers from 1842. This decade, the 1840s, marked the first land sales of Moreton Bay plots in Sydney and Brisbane.

Those who put the land to work did so roughly in sequence, exhausting the possibilities of specific enterprises as resources ran short or limitations became clear. The *Sydney Colonist* in 1835 described Moreton Bay as extensive and 'abounding with the finest fish, including turtles, &c., and four navigable streams', being the rivers Brisbane, Logan and Tweed and Scotts Creek. The last three of these, noted the correspondent, were abundant with cedar, which was felled and milled by convict workers and returned to Dunwich as lumber – Dunwich being the name then given to the prospective city attached to the penal settlement at Brisbane.

The article commends the suitability of the river planes to 'tobacco, cotton, and the sugar-cane, [which] can be cultivated to any extent, with the prospect of a copious return.'[2] The tone of the article is unashamedly boosterish, encouraging entrepreneurship and speculative settlement with the promise of strong returns on any agricultural venture to which the newcomer might turn his hand. That this same issue of the *Colonist* announced, too, the establishment of the free settlement at South Australia, is a signal of the newspaper's readership: those on the lookout for new prospects within the system of the empire in which to turn territory to profit.

Settlers of the five shires that would (wholly or in part) in 1949 combine to form Albert Shire (Nerang, Tingalpa, Beenleigh, Coomera and Waterford) would over the first half-century's systematic settlement in turn explore the possibilities of cotton, tobacco, sugar, and arrowroot. Some crops would enjoy temporary success, while others would endure as staples of the region's economy. The rivers not only defined the nature of the soil and shaped the topography. They also offered this first generation of farmers and timber-getters a ready transportation system for moving goods around, and for sending to mill that timber cleared in order to turn land to agriculture. As in the cane fields that once covered what is now the Isle of Capri, this layer has over the course of the last century been thoroughly overwritten by suburban sprawl and the extension of the city's infrastructure to service it. But in the nineteenth and early twentieth centuries, today's chic inner-urban suburbs were on farming land.

Holthouse succinctly rehearses the story of how the Gold Coast was first opened up to timber extraction. 'About 1842', he writes, 'with the Tweed county becoming too crowded, two young timber getters, Edmund Harper and William Duncan, scaled the McPherson Range to the headwaters of the Nerang River [then, and until the 1860s, called the Barrow River]. They followed it down to the sea and, just downstream from where Little Tallebudgera Creek joined it and made it broad enough for a rafting area, Harper built a humpy and wharf.'[3] This, he suggests, was the first British dwelling in the area behind present-day Surfers Paradise. The earthworks to drain the Great Swamp and realise Florida Gardens, along with the sequence of canal estates built in their wake, dramatically reshaped the topography that Harper and Duncan encountered more than a century earlier. But as we observed in the previous chapter, Cascade Gardens stands on a long-established site on which the local peoples met and fished. Harper is buried in an informal grave somewhere therein. Over the course of his lifetime, however, timber extraction ran much of its full course. Michael Jones recalls that present-day Queensland was noted for the variety of its timber species, boasting as many variations as New South Wales and the area around Port Phillip (later Victoria) combined. Timber-getters quickly followed the path purportedly beaten by Harper and Duncan across the 1840s, putting Harper's wharf to good use. They supplied mills established at Southport and Tweed Heads as well as in Brisbane and further afield.[4] At the midpoint between the mouth of the Nerang and Tweed rivers, on the Tallebudgera Creek, timber extractors were recorded as being at work in Burleigh Heads (then called Burly) in 1858, which marked a saturation, of sorts, and opened the door to a new set of economic drivers.

In a telling assessment of climatic and topographical verisimilitude, the planes of the territory's rivers were assessed to be well suited to farming cotton, as had already been suggested in the 1830s, and the first efforts to do so from the end of the 1850s were deemed a success. The Reverend John Lang had promoted Queensland's prospects in Britain as, to quote the subtitle of his 1861 book on the subject, *A Highly Eligible Field for Emigration and the Future Cotton Field of Great Britain*.[5] The disruption of the international cotton trade caused by the outbreak of the American Civil War in 1861 fuelled the promise for Queensland of profiting from cotton harvests that had been positively assessed in Great Britain a year earlier. A sales poster (fig. 3.2) depicts land parcels on the Nerang River that had been held by the Manchester Cotton Company since the early 1860s, when entrepreneurs Edmund H. Price and G. Britten owned nearly 800 hectares in the area of present-day Bundall – the

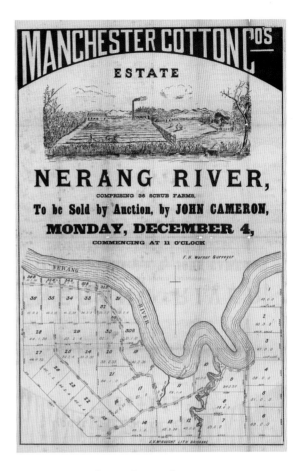

3.2 Manchester Cotton Company's Estate, Nerang River, 1882.

setting, today, of the Gold Coast Cultural Precinct – and Carrara, further upriver where a large stadium sits, opposite the late-1990s Nifsan development of Emerald Lakes.

The map documents the region's participation in the Industrial Revolution, a world apart from the Lancastrian factory towns, but for a spell indispensable to their production. Large landholdings were acquired, too, by Robert Towns around the Logan River in 1862. Present-day Veresdale, near Beaudesert, was originally Townsvale; this is not to be confused with Townsville in the state's north, which he also founded. Within three years of the foundation of Queensland's first cotton

3.3 Naïve drawing of Captain Towns's 'Townsvale' Cotton Plantation, Veresdale, c.1865.

plantation in 1861, the Caboolture Cotton Company, the list of applicants for land for this purpose had become extensive, reflecting an industry at its local peak, shortly to be undermined by flooding and a series of destructive frosts; and the return of American production to its full capacity.[6] Thomas Hanlon was among the colonial immigrants sponsored to establish and develop plantations on the Logan River planes, and he would have a significant hand in later developments in the region. Pacific Islanders and Aboriginal workers were taken on as field labourers (fig. 3.3). Cotton was quickly replaced in the 1860s by sugar, which drew on the same plantation logic as the cotton fields and redeployed the population of conscripted workers from the Melanesian islands whose efforts had, from 1863, come to underpin the entire operation. Of the cotton industry, little remains barring the logic of early farm plots and such artefacts as the name of Gin House Creek, behind Broadbeach.

At its peak in 1872, the sugar industry of today's Gold Coast hinterland, extending up to the Logan River, contributed a quarter of Queensland's substantial sugar production, but by the end of the 1880s it had reached its nadir, having become overextended and sufficiently underdeveloped to sustain changes in the international market. It also became a victim, ultimately, both of changing labour laws that had begun to eliminate the exploitative

treatment of Melanesian workers and a depression that settled across Queensland in the early 1890s. Large communities of Pacific Islanders had built up around the region's agriculture and in the 1881 census amounted to a full tenth of the population of the Logan district.[7] With the advent of the White Australia policy stance on labour in the first years of Federation, this sizeable population would be expelled and any remaining farmers would need to rely on domestic workers, and pay them a fair wage. The economic challenges to nineteenth-century landholdings, however, did not yet lie with changing labour laws so much as shifts in the economies in which they sought to participate and local weather challenges that had, in a small number of severe cases, caught the plantations off guard.

Holthouse suggests the longer-term consequences for the city of this first, failed plantation industry: 'Many who had originally come to the South Coast to grow cotton, took up land to go farming. They clustered together for mutual support and small townships began to grow up, many of them on the sites of old stockyards and outstations. Some went in for the cultivation of arrowroot and, at White's old out-station of Pimpama, Francis Lahey built a mill for processing it.'[8] Alongside the cultivation of arrowroot at Pimpama, the Queensland colonial government sponsored the establishment of sugar cane plantations and sugar mills along the banks of the major rivers south of Brisbane (figs 3.4 and 3.5). The region's agriculture extended, by the end of the century, to include

3.4 Sketch of the Benowa Sugar Plantation homestead and cane fields, Benowa, c.1886.

3.5 Boyd's horse-powered sugar mill with
worker, Ormeau, 1873.

3.6 Pine Mountain sawmill, Numindah
Valley, Queensland, which was owned by
the Yaun family, c.1880.

maize, bananas, grapes, potatoes and hay, none of
which secured its prosperity. Quite the contrary.[9]
The scale of the operations, as Jones has noted
elsewhere, supported self-contained communities
with such amenities as a hotel and stores, and
sometimes a post office serviced by the Cobb and
Co. carriages.[10] Mills continued to process timber
right past the turn of the century, increasingly
supplying the lumber needed to build the industrial
structures and houses needed for the region's
growing population (figs 3.6 and 3.7).

By the 1880s, many of the first-generation
plantation landholdings had been turned over to
cattle farming. Jones recalls the lease names of the
largest cattle runs in the Albert and Logan regions
at the start of the 1860s: Moondoolum, Albert and
Logan Rivers, Pimpama, Nindooimba, Tamborine
and Bromelton. Together they comprised nearly
190,000 acres of land (760 square kilometres) and
more than 20,000 head of cattle (for the most part)
and sheep.[11] It was a substantial industry from
the foundation of the colony of Queensland and
remained important through to the twentieth
century. The Queensland Government in 1889
bolstered the region's dairy industry by introducing
a travelling training centre that brought farms up to
speed with the most recent technological advances.[12]
The sight even today of cattle feeding alongside
the large roundabout at Mudgeeraba, just a few
minutes' drive from Pacific Fair in Broadbeach, is

3.7 Schneider's sawmill and workers,
Waterford, c.1898.

3.8 William Laver's Dairy Farm 'Red Hill',
Mudgeeraba, 1910.

an apt reminder of the contemporary vestiges of the long-standing role of dairy farming in the region's economic and cultural life (fig. 3.8). Its prominence has, however, largely faded with time. The Vievers house ('Somerset', fig. 3.9) is memorably captured by turn-of-the-century photography, and recorded in the family history as a dwelling made of red cedar with floors of clean huon pine and joinery of oak – studs of three metres' height, and views commanding the Merrimac countryside. The Schmidt farmhouse and outbuildings survive from this era, having been built at Worongary in stages since 1880 and now located on the edge of the Mudgeeraba Showgrounds. In Willow Vale, the farmhouse at Laurel Hill, an arrowroot farm, was built in Ruffles Road in 1883–84 by one Alex Fortune, and reminds us in its endurance of the overlapping layers of agriculture across what would for half a century be the Albert Shire. Other farmhouses of the 1860s, 1870s and 1880s survive in photographs or, as in the case of the 1861 Boowaggan Cottage, in replica.

The important point to make, though, is that the earliest colonial Gold Coast settlements were not the seaside towns of the late-nineteenth century but the trading and industry towns that preceded them by a generation or more.

Jones has observed that the 'gung-ho' attitudes underpinning the first waves of agricultural settlement took little heed of the region's sometimes delicate ecology, and made few efforts to understand how its original peoples had worked with the land. While the 1860s and 1870s had enjoyed a period of good climatic conditions, the settlers had failed to understand this as a departure from the area's

3.9 Veivers family in the garden at 'Talgai Homestead', Mudgeeraba, c.1900.

3.10 A sketch of the Pimpama Hotel, Pimpama, 1874.

normal weather patterns, with their cycles of heavy rainfall and flooding. The logic of removing vast forests as a protection against flooding failed as soon as the weather returned to its regular habits. Settlers were reminded of the origins of the regions numerous rivers with a number of major floods from 1887 onwards, undermining agriculture and hampering efforts to establish bridges and wharfs to maintain the connections between inland settlements that had been established to that point.[13]

A drawing from 1874 (fig. 3.10) by hotel proprietor J. W. Drewe of his own premises in Pimpama, for example, documents a lively town that enjoyed constant custom as a node on the Cobb and Co. route south of Brisbane. While Southport would eventually eclipse settlements like Pimpama, it had only been surveyed a year before Drewe put pen to paper, and had yet to see a land sale. These service towns were tied closely to the agriculture and industries of their districts and formed part of a large network of towns spanning from Brisbane to the border. Even if they were difficult to maintain and at the mercy of the weather, they formed an inland commercial infrastructure, serviced by ferries, coach and (from 1872) steamers, that thoroughly preceded the more famous developments that would transpire from the end of the nineteenth century. A series of bridges was built from the mid-1870s onwards to replace the ferry services that had operated to that point that have been successively replaced over the decades as transport has changed in both mode and density. Bridges at Yatala and Waterford were both built in 1876 (although both, too, were tested and found wanting in the flood of 1887). The Logan Railway Bridge followed in 1885.

The town of Beenleigh had regular stagecoach connections to Brisbane and Waterford (largely abandoned, and now a suburb of Logan city), with lodges, clubs and societies, a full complement of churches, banks and a court – all this for a population of 400 (many of whom being German, rather than British immigrants). The postal townships of Coomera, Nerang and Logan were all similarly well equipped. 'At the end of 1875', recalled Lena Cooper in her 1946 memoir, 'the Coomera and Nerang State Schools were the only schools between Beenleigh and New South Wales.'[14] (Southport followed, in 1879.) Other towns, like Tamborine and Yatala, had more basic amenities, but clear anchors to their working and civic life – a tobacco factory and racecourse respectively. Benowa and Veresdale are exceptions. With only twenty-five people living in Benowa in 1876, it nonetheless had its own police station and courthouse, a hotel, blacksmith, general store and butcher – substantially better equipped than nearby Nerang, perhaps the most formal of the early towns. (Nerang had been surveyed by Martin Lavelle in 1865, but much of the land was undeveloped; and the town was known primarily for its taverns, like the Royal Mail, opened in 1874.) Veresdale, too, was well set to service its largely agricultural population, but this was thoroughly dependent on the extensive Towns plantation. The distribution of hotels across the nineteenth-century Gold Coast reflects the distribution of pockets of trade and industry while reflecting, too, the growing importance of the hinterland towns for communications with the southern colonies. The Queen's Hotel (fig. 3.11) dates back to a time, in the 1880s, when coaches needed regular rest stops. William Kennedy's decision to build the Queen's close to the proposed Nerang Railway Station captures, too, the coincidence of this network with the rail system that would shortly make it redundant. So, too, the march of technical progress

3.11 Queen's Hotel with Cobb and Co. coach outside, Nerang c.1890.

and the possibility of national networks were presaged by the construction of a telegraph office in Nerang in 1875, directing communications between Queensland's colonial capital and New South Wales.

By the end of the 1870s, Southport had a clear profile as a settlement and a population to match the largest of the future Gold Coast's agricultural and plantation townships. Its steady traffic of well-heeled visitors from Brisbane prompted improvements of the roadways, river crossings and amenities between the Logan and Nerang rivers. The first building in present-day Southport had been raised on the site of what was from 1901 to 2016 the Star of the Sea Convent. Orientated not towards the Broadwater but inland, it was the outstation of one of the large, early sheep farms, owned by William Duckett White. The outstation did, of course, overlook the water, as would the house, Warraby, which White built in the 1850s, but rather than marking an arrival at the seaside, they were more like the distant extensions of the main business of agriculture, the heart of which was inland. For farmers like White, the separation of the colony of Queensland and the regularisation of land speculation and selection that followed in its wake changed the patterns and pace of settlement. As Holthouse has observed, the river planes were quickly snapped up for various kinds of farm and plantation, and he quotes White in saying that 'the selectors took all the best river flats and left us with the hills.'[15] (That

3.12 Thomas Hanlon's Ferry Hotel, Yatala, 1872.

said, White still owned the Coombabah Run through to the 1860s, encompassing all of Southport and Nerang Heads, or present-day Labrador.)

Thomas Hanlon (introduced above) went to work for White when the cotton industry failed, eventually establishing himself at Yatala, on the Albert River. His ferry service across the river gave the name to his Ferry Hotel (fig. 3.12), which joined a network of hotels ensuring greater communication and mobility across the sprawling planes – supported principally, at first, by a thriving sugar industry, but also ensuring an open path from Brisbane to Nerang and other townships further south. In fact, he built the hotel in 1871, a year after he had established a post office on that site to service the region's sugar estates. With a foot inland, he remained a frequent vacationer to Nerang Heads into the 1870s. When the area was surveyed into one-acre blocks by G. L. Pratten in 1874, it was purportedly Hanlon who suggested the name of Southport, which adhered. Hanlon himself bought one of the twenty-two blocks that sold in 1875, and alongside his own house he founded the Pacific Hotel, which he enlarged by adding a second storey in 1878. In making the transition from agriculture to hospitality, Hanlon was not alone: Frederick Fowler had started extracting timber on his land in Mudgeeraba in 1869 before establishing the Burleigh Heads Hotel in 1882, for many years an important stop on the coastal expeditions undertaken by holiday-makers who had made their way from Brisbane by means of

Southport. In Southport itself, the first house was built by Robert Johnston, who had likewise bought a share of the acre lots but built his house on a more elevated site, naming it Balclutha. He, too, had done his time on the farm, at Pimpama.

In recalling the first of these settlers at Southport, Holthouse names them one after the other as they established the amenities of a nineteenth-century town, and the bases for its future: a tavern, hotels, butcher, mill, and so forth.[16] Southport was, however, not even mentioned in the 1876 edition of *Bailliere's Queensland Gazetteer and Road Guide*, the entries in which Jones handily summarises in *Country of Five Rivers*.[17] It retained much of the character of the uncultivated Nerang Heads into the 1880s, when it began to experience a decisive and irreversible transition to seaside resort. But this did not happen suddenly. Nor did those landholdings that had turned Nerang, Waterford and their various neighbours – close to a dozen shires in all – from a settlement prospect in the colonial mould into a territory participating in economies at a range of scales.

A turn-of-the-century photograph in Nerang shows a horse-drawn cart bearing three sizeable logs, pulled up outside the Commercial Hotel. A sign peeking out behind the felled timber advertises the local branch of the Commercial Bank of New South Wales (fig. 3.13). This captures as well as any image the interchange between natural

3.13 Logs pulled by a horse team, resting in front of the Commercial Hotel, Nerang, Gold Coast, *c*.1900.

3.14 Parishes of Coomera and Barrow, 1884–1890.

resources, financial structures, local commerce and regional infrastructure that underpinned the Gold Coast's nineteenth-century industrial history – without which Southport and the seaside may have developed along entirely different lines. The fabric of these overlapping enterprises forms the basis of the Gold Coast's settler architectural and industrial heritage. As lines on a survey map, however, or timbers left undisturbed by the changes surrounding them, architecture also emerges from this history as a kind of analogue as much as it does a field of technical expertise, or as a set of ideas. Surveys of land in the 1880s (figs 3.14 and 3.15) describe large composite landholdings in private hands and in those of such banks as the Commercial Bank of New South Wales, the Commercial Banking Co. of Sydney, and the Commercial Bank of Australia, all of which

3.15 Parishes of Pimpama and Cedar, 1884–1890.

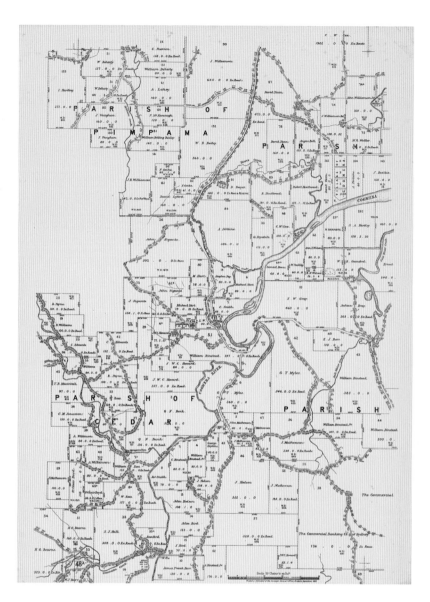

facilitated the investment in farms, plantations and residential blocks over several decades. In this sense, the shape applied by the surveyor's hand to the country that had been worked and lived in on an entirely different logic for thousands of years engaged in a constant conversation with the modest branches of the first continent-wide banks, and with the farmers of various crops and stock who in turn fed their vaults and, over time, fed off them (fig. 3.16).

By the twentieth century, the region had effectively resolved the encounter between the beach and hinterland by way of a negotiated split. On one hand, in those sparsely populated parishes and shires that would at the end of the 1940s form the Albert Shire, a dairy industry interspersed among residual plantations for sugar and arrowroot was effectively awaiting the advent of suburban sprawl. The artefacts of the nineteenth-century experience of what would become the Gold

3.16 The Commercial Bank of Australia,
Scarborough Street, Southport, *c.*1900
(postcard).

Coast – inland, and to the north – including those farmhouses and industrial buildings, hotels and churches, marked fleeting moments of industry and commerce that have been overtaken by the modern city, even as they fought to stay alive as the city crept out to meet them. This was once the land of 'a hard-working frontier society where few had any time to play on the beach.'[18] But the beach emerged from the nineteenth century front and centre as an image, even if, as an immediate reality, it remained distant for many. As such, the present-day city results, in part, from a moment in which the beach itself, and hence the South Coast, became ascendant. In this, the agricultural infrastructure of the nineteenth century was obliged to give way to the infrastructure of rest and the temptations of speculation on a modern form of recreation.

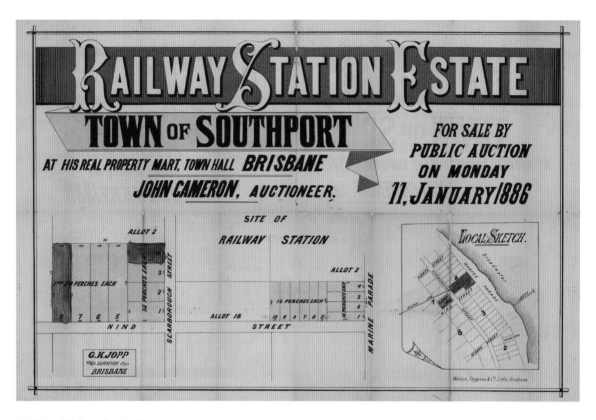

4.1 Map of Railway Station Estate,
Southport, 1886.

4   On the Beach

The iconic view of the Gold Coast is its shoreline; the bank of high-rise hotels and apartment buildings testifying to the pull of the sand. It was not always so, however, and the shift in attention from the farm lands and plantations to the beach is one of the irreversible changes to which the towns and shires that combined to form South Coast after the Second World War were subject in their nineteenth-century infancy. The topographical features noted by James Cook in his voyage of 1770 reference the respect with which the ocean was long regarded – Point Danger, Mount Warning – and as we have seen, the first settlers to reach the sea did so from inland. Notwithstanding the long-standing importance of Moreton Bay and the Pacific Coast for the original Gold Coasters, the elevation of the seaside as a site of recreation for nineteenth-century settlers owes much to broad shifts in attitude across the eighteenth and nineteenth centuries, with the manifest rise in Britain of towns like Brighton, Blackpool, Scarborough and Lytham St Annes during the reign of Victoria and her successors, in response to the free time introduced into family life by the greater regulation of workplaces and vacations and the advent of the Bank Holiday. Britain's own Southport, too, figured prominently among the seaside towns, having offered Liverpudlians the chance to take a day or two at the beach since the 1790s. There is little coincidence, then, that Queensland's Southport (first surveyed in 1874 and incorporated in 1918) became an important setting for recreation in the colony's south-east corner – after its initial establishment as a port and site of commerce, collecting, milling and shipping timber, with the construction of the first pier in 1884, a setting for seaside vacations and, hence, an index of widespread cultural change.

The pier first allowed passenger boats to bring visitors south from Brisbane on a daily steam service, with the introduction of the Beenleigh-Southport rail line extension in 1889 making the passage south from the capital more straightforward. (A second pier followed in 1914, once the town's reputation was thoroughly established.) The event marking the opening of that railway typified the dual uses to which Southport was often put (figs 4.1 and 4.2). As much

4.2 Opening of the Southport Railway Station, 24 January 1898.

4.3 Surfers Paradise beach, 1880.

a celebration of the settlement's coming of age, it also declared its importance to the network of settlements in the colony's south-east. It had not yet achieved the status of a town, but the rail connection made clear the impending fortunes of this small, thriving settlement. The *Brisbane Courier* reported that upon the arrival of the 'Ministerial party' to inaugurate the line and partake in official proceedings, 'the majority of the visitors, of whom there could not have been less than 500 or 600, spread themselves out along the various reaches and other resorts, and employed themselves in picnicking.'[1] For these visitors, Southport's reputation as a vacation setting had already been established and the rail made it easier to access those amenities, both natural and commercial that equipped it to serve the region to these ends. (Once established, the Southport Express from Brisbane to Tweed – today approximately an hour by car at average speeds – still meant a substantial four-hour journey.)

A report in that same newspaper six years earlier, indicates how far Southport had come in the meantime in securing that reputation – the roads being more difficult at the start of the 1880s. Already Southport's possibilities had been noted.

A correspondent named T. P. S. (S.) describes 'A Trip to Southport and Burleigh Heads' in February 1883, travelling from the town of Beenleigh by horseback through fields given over to sugar cane, maize and (at Pimpama) arrowroot, as well as to cattle grazing. The author writes of setting his sights on 'the blue and green waves curling over each other in their race for the shore', and this after a fourteen-year absence from the town (which puts his last visit to the coast well before Southport was even surveyed, and when the area was called Nerang Creek Heads). 'I was much struck', he notes, 'with the bustle and go-aheadism of the place, everyone seeming to be in a tremendous hurry.' Southport's growth had continued to match that of Brisbane in those same years, then, with amenities abounding, as the correspondent recounts: 'three excellent hotels, four stores, a State school, and a very large building for a private school, belonging to Mrs Davenport [relocated in 1882 from Ipswich]; a reserve for recreation ground, paled in, on which improvements were being made for a lawn tennis and cricket ground; a telegraph office, court-house, police station, savings bank, &c.' Added to this were the makings of a music hall, under construction, and a Roman Catholic chapel, also under construction – both stalled for want of the timber necessary to keep up with demand. The Congregationalists, Anglicans and Presbyterians had their churches already (all in Nerang Street). 'Land has advanced tremendously in value these three or four years past, and at present well-situated allotments are selling rapidly and at extraordinary prices.' (As much as £25 per acre!) The Cobb & Co. terminus at the Labrador Hotel places visitors squarely on the beach at the Broadwater (as it was by then called); and Mrs Beetham's two-storey 'Woodlands' guest house offers a fine view of the same. The roads are rough but in the process of being improved. Our correspondent asserts: 'Southport, to my mind, has a great future before it. With its splendid beach, its beautiful scenery, its boating, fishing, and shooting, its comparative proximity to Brisbane, with its almost daily steamers to and fro and last, but not least its respectable and pushing residents, it only requires population and railway communications with Brisbane to make it a second Newport or Brighton.'[2]

Despite the importance of timber milling for the foundations of the settlement (Robert Johnson

Nerang Street, Southport, looking East.

4.4 Coloured postcard of Nerang Street,
Southport, c.1890.

established the first mill in 1876), it seems that local supply could not meet the demand. One sawmiller, a Mr R. Muir, indicated to the correspondent his intention to move his operation (one of the two or three then in operation at Southport) closer to the more thickly timbered area of Labrador. Between Labrador and Southport, notes S., are many stumps indicating houses started but stalled.[3]

While Southport offered a serene and well-serviced setting for a seaside holiday, access to the Pacific surf at Coolangatta, at the state border, or Burleigh, half-way there on the journey from Southport, was hampered by the need to cross the Nerang River. Before the Jubilee Bridge was built in 1925 allowing ready vehicular access to the beach, the journey described by S. was perhaps more typical. He writes that he was one of a party of twenty who set out towards Burleigh, meeting a group of men who were trying to get the ferry, operated by a sugar mill owner named Johann

Meyer, into the water – it having been stranded above the waterline by a high tide. (Meyer's Ferry gave its name to Southport's Ferry Road, the crossing somewhat obscured by mid-century canal developments, but now a bridge over the Nerang.) Once across, a ride over rough terrain and through heavy scrub was rewarded with 'a view of magnificent grandeur ... Before us the ocean lay in all its beauty, with the summer sun reflected on its surface; to the left and right of us a splendid beach of hard white sand with the breakers rolling in at our very feet.' They carried on, then, to Burleigh – distinguished by its 'bold hill rising most abruptly from the sea, splendidly grassed, the beautiful colour of which, contrasted with the still deeper green of the scrub which crowns its summit, and the deep blue of the mingled with the green of the ocean underneath, gives a *tout ensemble* at once magnificent and beautiful.' The sole guesthouse at Burleigh as of 1883 was sited to capture this view

4.5 Burleigh Hotel, Burleigh Heads, c.1900.

– the Burleigh Hotel (fig. 4.5) owned by the timber-getter Frederick Fowler.[4]

This account describes a town that was already well established and ready for what would follow. A notice in that same issue of the *Courier* advertised the fifth annual Southport Regatta. But even so, between the article by S. in the *Brisbane Courier*

and the opening of the Southport Railway five years later, the population had increased nearly three-fold (350 in 1884, with 80 houses, to a neat 1,000 in 1889). It had grown quickly from the time that Richard Gardner had built the first house there (in 1869) to offer increased infrastructure to allow a dual-speed economy offering services to the extraction and agriculture industries and amenities to tourists. James Tuesley, who had been a whaler, built a cutter called *Witch of the Creek*, which made weekly return journeys between Brisbane and Nerang. Other services added to the regularity of the journeys between Southport and Brisbane, but barely. In both cases, the settlement supported the work of turning natural resources to profit.

Southport's fortunes were held to have increased due to the tacit endorsement of the town by the Governor of Queensland, Sir Anthony Musgrave, who served in that post from 1883 to 1888. Musgrave spent his summers in Southport, and his house (now called Biddle House, fig. 4.7) remains on its original site: now the grounds of the Southport School. The coincidence between Southport's growth and Musgrave's tenure are worth exploring,

SOUTHPORT, BAR, Q.

4.6 Coloured postcard of Southport Pier looking east from Star of the Sea Convent, c.1900.

4.7 The Southport School viewed from
the Nerang River, c.1908.

social mores informing beach etiquette and its
most famous breaches; the seaside activities and
the social history they have informed. A series of
civic buildings by the Brisbane firm of Hall and
Phillips, all in an art deco style, survive as markers
of Southport's coming of age: the bathing pavilions
at Main Beach (fig. 4.8) and Southport (both 1934),
the Southport Surf Lifesaving Club (completed in
1936), and, most significantly, a fine new town hall
(fig. 4.9), which was completed in 1935 and replaced
a timber structure that had been built in 1919.
These buildings overwrote a layer of civic buildings
realised to meet the new demands placed on the
settlement prior to its incorporation as a town,

but it would be an error to place the town's late
nineteenth-century successes at his feet alone.
Musgrave was not so much a catalyst for a boom
in the real estate market as confirmation that
the town could serve individuals of high social
standing. No longer a frontier town, Southport
was at the avant-garde of a rush to the ocean
precipitated by increasingly better roads and
more democratic access to the means to make
the journey south. It was also at the forefront of a
wave of developments specifically aimed at those
who valued the seaside. The trains that flooded
Southport with day-trippers both well-heeled and
undesirable, provided from the 1890s onwards a
measure of security against economic fluctuations
in those industries on which the first generation of
Southport residents had depended.

The region's recreational culture has been subject
to both history and myth, capturing the shifting

4.9 Southport Town Hall,
1930s.

and then afterwards. They also added a new set
of buildings attending specifically to the seaside,
complementing the various amusements on the pier
and along the edge of the Broadwater.

Much had changed across the region now
occupied by the Gold Coast between the 1890s
and the 1930s.[5] The Jubilee Bridge had made
travel to the southern settlements of Burleigh and
Coolangatta significantly easier. A Coolangatta
Town Council had been formed in 1914, but it took
the influenza epidemic of 1919 to prompt its own
rapid growth – limitations on travel rendered the
border a hard, southern boundary for Queensland.
It also prompted the need for separate amenities,

4.8 Main Beach Bathing Pavilion,
c.1936.

4.10 Pacific Ocean Estate sales advertisement, 1915.

including a school, post office and churches, for which Coolangatta residents had relied on the services of its conjoined twin of Tweed Heads in New South Wales for some years.[6] And Burleigh had sought to exploit its position at the centre of the two otherwise distant settlements. Further north and west, the farming lands remained productive, but towns that were thriving in the nineteenth century began to languish as routes diverted travellers towards the coast and frequent services by rail and sea circumvented altogether those towns that had once supported the journey by land. Even in Southport, the lack of a town water supply extended to 1932, while sewerage remained a perennial issue into the 1960s.

Over these interwar years, the city's centre of gravity moved steadily towards the Pacific Coast, with the real estate development of Elston as much of a focus now as it would continue to be as Surfers Paradise. Elston was built up around a strip of land between the Nerang River and the beach settled in the 1860s. As Hector Holthouse recalls, the timber-getters Jim Beattie and Jim Miller built a large house on the site now occupied by the Tiki Village. The site was accessible by Meyer's ferry, but also by boat services from Southport.[7] The area just north of Elston was surveyed and sold in 1915 as the Pacific Ocean Estate (fig. 4.10). In 1925, the Cavills bought land on which they raised the Elston Hotel. A modest start, it was quickly expanded with the construction of the Elston Surf Life Saving Club. Both were rebranded by the end of the decade as the Surfers Paradise Hotel and Surf Life Saving Club, reflecting the growing interwar popularity of the pastime.[8] When the hotel burned down in 1936, it was quickly replaced in a complex that was extended to include a zoo, gardens and accommodation. Cavill's original establishment was thereby superseded by an art deco hotel designed in 1937 by the highly regarded Trewern partnership of Brisbane (demolished 1983, now Centro Surfers Paradise). The municipal borders proposed by the Royal Commission on Local Government Boundaries in 1928 included the settlement of Elston within the sprawling and largely inland Nerang Shire, bordered to the north and south by the smaller, but more densely populated towns of Southport and Coolangatta. Across this decade, though, and into the next, one patch of seaside land after the next was transformed into real estate and quietly occupied. The settlement of Elston was by no means quiet,

4.11 Surfers Paradise Hotel at Elston, c.1928.

4.12 Surfers Paradise Surf Lifesaving
Clubhouse, erected in 1931.

4.13 Quiet street scene in Cavill Avenue,
Surfers Paradise, c.1938.

though, but when reporters could describe the
Cavills' hotel as a popular spot some distance from
town, there was little sense that in time this would
become the symbolic centre of the city: not just a
pub, but an approximation of the Gold Coast entire.

In 1935 the South Coast's beaches had also
become a resource of another kind. The coastal edge
had been put to work by the introduction of sand-
mining, which by the 1950s had, in Currumbin and
Broadbeach, 'already compromised the ecology of
the Gold Coast, so canal builders had no difficulty
in converting mangroves into canal estates.'[9]
The process was brutal, permanently altering
the mineral makeup of the beaches, promoting
erosion through the removal of dune grass and
those elements that had bound the dunes together.
In a sense, however, it was exposing the region to
an industrial procedure that paralleled, through
physical interventions in the environment, the
transformation of the beach into a resource for the
national tourist industry. In his contribution to
the catalogue *Flesh*, Peter Spearritt observed that
the 'Gold Coast has some of the most constantly
redeveloped real estate anywhere in Australia.'[10] That
this is true owes much to the apparent discovery of
the beach – these beaches – across the 1930s.

Their qualities were confirmed during the
Second World War by the establishment of

recreational camps for US servicemen. While the
Pacific Command was headquartered in the newly
completed buildings of Queensland University,
the US Navy Recreational Bases at Kirra Beach and
Green Mount (Coolangatta) saw a steady flow of
American personnel unwinding at the beach.

By the war's end, then, and with a period of
prosperity coinciding with the fresh ubiquity of
the family car, the South Coast had been firmly
established in the national consciousness as
a resort town, a place in which to step away
and unwind – not just for Queenslanders and
the farmers of the Darling Downs, but for the

4.14 Kirra Surf Life Saving Club, Kirra
Beach, c.1946.

4.15 Tarzana Travelotel, Coolangatta
(1949), *c.*1950.

populous southern states of New South Wales
and Victoria. This image absorbed successive
and competing layers of the city's history, which
had been filed behind the image of the city that
had been emerging across the first half of the
twentieth century and which was formalised

during the war itself. It was advanced not only in
the environments described by Robin Boyd in *The
Australian Ugliness* and quoted in this book's first
pages, but by a specific type of building: the motel,
as new to the 1940s as the guest house had been to
the 1880s. From the end of the 1940s motels began

to proliferate along the coastal strip, providing for those who arrived into Surfers Paradise and its neighbouring settlements not by train or boat, but by car. Invoking life in southern California, the Tarzana Travelotel (fig. 4.15) was opened in 1949, the first of the Gold Coast's motels and quickly followed by several dozen establishments responding to the shrinking travel times between locations, especially to the south, that had previously made travel prohibitive to families. Monuments of this emerging national city include the El Dorado (designed by Douglas and Barnes, 1954) along with a string of names more evocative in their name and signage than compelling in their design and amenity: the El Rancho, Florida Car-o-tel, Santa Fe and Pineapple Motel – all opened in the 1960s.

They were accompanied by a mid-1950s building boom that was widely reported in the press and in trade journals. As we will soon see, the boom required innovative thinking to conjure real estate from the most unlikely sources in a setting where it appeared to be in limited supply. But all that followed described a fundamental change in the way that the South Coast had been conceived – a change in which the Gold Coast, as a city, and as an idea, was lying latent.

5.1 Aerial view of Surfers Paradise
with the Surfers Paradise Hotel in the
foreground, *c.*1950.

5 Gold on the Sand

In the run-up to the Queensland centenary year of 1959, *Architecture in Australia* dedicated a portion of the January–March 1958 issue to the architecture of Queensland. In his editorial remarks, Queensland Government Architect Edward Weller (signing as E. J. W.) argued for a hitherto unrecognised depth in the work of the state's architects: 'It could be that by the measure of Sydney or Melbourne, Queensland architecture may seem to progress backward rather than forward … [but] Queensland architects seem bold enough to design for Queensland's needs. May they succeed in their purpose!'[1] Three articles follow: Morton Herman surveying the efforts of the Department of Public Works; Neville Lund presenting a first assessment of the life and work of arts and crafts architect Robin S. Dods; and E. J. (Eddie) Hayes turning the reader's attention to the Town of South Coast – which would formally become the Town of Gold Coast on October 23 of that year, and the City of Gold Coast on May 16, 1959.[2] The velocity of change is, ultimately, Hayes's theme in this brief reflection on the nature of architectural practice in a town in which the future was very much undetermined.

'Up to 1945', writes Hayes, 'Surfers remained a relatively quiet place. Most of the roads were unformed, life was informal, and most of the houses were week-enders owned by Brisbane families. With a few exceptions the buildings were crude, badly planned and uncomfortable, wherein people seemed to vie with one another to achieve the ultimate in ugliness and discomfort. Some of these buildings have survived, but most of them have been moved to less expensive areas or have been demolished.' The town, suggests Hayes, was built on a culture of speculation and risk, for which the shifting sands of its dunes were an apt metaphor. Jim Cavill's 'small hotel drowsing on the sand dunes of the South Queensland coast' sowed the seeds for what could already, in 1958, be described as 'a tourist empire of sand, sun and gold' (fig. 5.1). Hayes recalls the settlement and development of Elston before turning to the crux of the matter. The casual had been traded for the intentioned in the emergence of the towns that would in 1949 form the municipality of the South Coast, combined, in turn, with Albert Shire to form the city that would nearly a half century later form the present-day Gold Coast. What had once been spontaneous, even accidental, was in the 1950s becoming increasingly deliberate.

Central to this shift was the matter of real estate development, the behaviour of the real estate market, and their combined impact on the town's growth – something that would continue to shape the way the South Coast was embracing its future as the Gold Coast. Hayes follows the lines quoted at length above with an observation that some houses 'built pre-war at a cost of £300 on land worth £50 have been sold for as much as £15,000.' There is nothing surprising in this. The population had doubled from the mid-1930s to the mid-1940s (recorded at 13,888 in 1947, against 6,046 in 1933) and doubled again over the next decade, so that by 1961 the Gold Coast had a population of 31,796: a five-fold increase over two decades that fostered the inflated values of existing housing stock and encouraged speculators to exploit undeveloped land, both in the narrow strip between the beach and the river, and in the hitherto unusable marsh land that was transformed from the mid-1950s into real estate.[3] The boom in the region's population followed the pattern set by Queensland as a whole in the twenty-five years following its independence from New South Wales – a ten-fold increase, in that case, from around 30,000 people to 300,000, with new settlers flocking to the north as city amenities were installed and upgraded in response to demand, and colonial infrastructure and industry demonstrated its enduring worth. The growth of the Gold Coast followed this logic. Its tourism industry had been supported by experiments in property development and growth in real estate values. Neither would be immune to the economic cycles of booms and busts that followed the city through the decades to follow, but as at the end of the 1950s, the performance of neither sector determined the life or death of the town.

Even at the relatively small scale of the newly renamed Gold Coast in 1958, Hayes could observe: 'It is unfortunate that the present development has taken pace without the benefit of a proper plan. The town plan which was prepared immediately after the war [the South Coast Planning Scheme of 1953] merely prescribed the areas into which buildings of varying categories were zoned and was superimposed on the existing grid of roads, but in fairness it must be stated that it was quite impossible at that time to foretell the growth which has taken place.' The problem faced by the South Coast architect had been one of narrow plots ('nearly all the original subdivisions were in blocks with 33 feet frontages') and an absence of infrastructure (notably sewerage, a perennial issue in the town's management). The 1953 plan introduced zoning controls to moderate pockets of densification and to control the initial phase of high-rise development

5.2 Harvey Graham Beach House, Surfers Paradise, 1953 (architects Hayes and Scott).

– this before any building in Surfers Paradise had reached ten stories in height. 'Notwithstanding the difficulties,' Hayes continues, 'it is a stimulating experience to practice on the Coast. In the few years since the relaxation of building controls, which effectively stifled nearly all building, Surfers Paradise has changed tremendously.'[4]

Hayes recounts three distinct phases in building on the South Coast up to the time in which he wrote. The first, he noted, was 'the period of house-building, with standards improving quickly and the people surprisingly willing to accept contemporary ideas in planning and design' (fig. 5.2 and 5.3). (His next comment indicates the consequences of the popular extension of this freedom: 'Undoubtedly

5.3 Pfitzenmaier Beach House, Northcliffe, 1953 (architects Hayes and Scott).

5.4 Sunseeker Private Hotel, cnr Gold
Coast Highway and Palm Avenue, Surfers
Paradise, *c.*1950.

many of the ideas have been adopted with too great enthusiasm and too little discrimination by the large number of people who plan their own houses. At least they provide plenty of surprises!') Following this first turn-of-the-century wave of real estate speculation in Southport and Coolangatta came the 'construction of serviced rooms, apartments and flats ... which all somehow manage to incorporate the word "Sun" in their name' (figs 5.4 and 5.5). This phase of development he attributes to 'southern visitors who came for a holiday and decided to stay.' A third phase, he notes, traded the interests of the private individual for those of 'companies and syndicates who can finance the larger projects which makes economic use of the extravagantly priced land.'[5] Michael Jones would later put it like this: 'Big capital replaced the money of well-meaning amateurs.'[6] Of course, what were for Hayes 'land costs at an unbelievably high level' would be thoroughly out-scaled by what followed, but he names such beneficiaries of the situation

as Lennon's Broadbeach Hotel (completed in December 1956), Stanley Korman's Chevron Hotel (licenced from 1957, with paying guests from 1958) and the elaboration of the Surfers Paradise Hotel itself. 'Similar developments are announced *almost weekly*, and it is probable that in the near future Surfers Paradise will be growing upward like Miami, Florida, USA.'

5.5 Sun Tan holiday flats on the Gold
Coast Highway, Surfers Paradise, *c.*1960.

5.6 Car-a-Park Caravan Park (architects
Hayes and Scott), Gold Coast Highway,
Mermaid Beach, 1958.

As a firm, Hayes and Scott were implicated in this
development. Hayes managed a number of Gold
Coast projects, and designed a number of houses,
both speculative and bespoke, from the end of the
Second World War onwards. Andrew Wilson has
thoroughly documented their production, which
includes an early house for Hayes's parents in
Northcliffe (1946), a speculative 'coast house' on
the corner of Frederick Street and the Gold Coast
Highway, at Surfers Paradise (1946), the Cooper
House (Broadbeach, 1948), a beach house for Ethne
Pfitzenmaier at Northcliffe (1953), and another
for Harvey Graham, again on the corner of the
Gold Coast Highway and Genoa Street in Surfers
(1953) – all now demolished.[7] And the Car-a-Park
Motels at Mermaid Beach (1959, fig. 5.6) combines
their modernist architectural language with the
expectations of visitors. The Pfitzenmaier Beach
House (fig. 5.3) is a celebrated project among these
early architecturally designed houses, with its
distinctively modernist butterfly roof. It won the firm
the Queensland Award for Meritorious Architecture
– perhaps the earliest instance of a South Coast work

receiving such state recognition.[8] By the 1960s, they
would regularly receive commissions for new houses
on the Gold Coast, along both the beach and the
newly developed riverside.

They were not alone. Across these decades, such
firms as Douglas and Barnes realised a number
of houses and residences across the Coast as a
significant branch of their professional profile.
Notable among them is the Art Union competition
home on Chevron Island (fig. 5.7). The brokers
of the residential Torbreck tower built in the
Brisbane suburb of Highgate Hill sought to exploit

5.7 Scarborough Art Union prize home on
Chevron Island (architects Douglas and
Barnes), 1961.

the investment opportunities open to them in
repeating the project elsewhere, an article in the
Courier Mail in 1959 advertising larger, sleeker
versions of the original on Surfers Paradise
and Burleigh Heads (fig. 5.8) – hailing it as 'the
greatest single contribution to home development
in Queensland.' Writing in 1958, though, Hayes
wondered whether the Gold Coast could sustain
this level of development long term and where
architects might find traction there as purveyors
of new buildings. The six decades that followed

5.8 Sketch of Torbreck at Burleigh Heads (architects Job and Froud), 1959.

Levy House, Margulies House, and the Lutheran Church Manse, all designed for Southport sites across the 1950s, demonstrated his modernism in a way that would be confirmed in projects of greater importance to the city over that decade and into the next. So, too, would his suburban scheme for Koala Park (between Burleigh Heads and Palm Beach) into the 1960s. These modest projects had been predicated by his design for Jimbour Cottage (again in Southport), a modern bungalow whose design had been featured in a special issue of the *Architectural Review* (*AR*) dedicated to *The*

have partially answered this question, however from the perspective of 1958, Hayes could still pose it without a clear sense of what would follow: 'What is the future of the booming Gold Coast? Is there any security for the millions which are being ploughed into estate development in parcels of money ranging as high as two millions, for a fantasy of man-made integration of home sites and waterways? Apparently,' he concluded, 'the … analogy of Miami inspires confidence, for the money keeps rolling and continues to spread gold on the sand' (fig. 5.9).

The post-war architectural history of the Gold Coast tracks three levels of activity: those buildings realised in a modern idiom that resonate with the assumed modernity of the city entire; those buildings that would define the city's ambitions and help to achieve them; and those gestures not registering as architecture at all, but realised at the scale of the city or landscape.

Brisbane-based Karl Langer is something of an exception in this scene, operating across all three scales, from the object to the city. Discrete works of architecture like the Gold Coast Little Theatre, the

5.9 Aerial view of development of Chevron Island looking towards Bundall, 1958.

Architecture of Australia (1948), which helped to bring Langer to post-war prominence, and with it his later Gold Coast projects. Prime Minister J. B. (Ben) Chifley, introducing that same issue of the *AR*, assessed the nation's architectural culture in these words: 'Today in Australia we are planning on a nation-wide basis. We are planning out towns on the principle that towns are a combined social organism and … that towns should be built to suit our convenience. No longer will they be just

5.10 Aerial view over Broadbeach and
Lennon's Broadbeach Hotel, Broadbeach,
1960.

allowed to grow.'[9] The criticism levelled at the
Gold Coast by those writers who would turn their
attentions to the Gold Coast in the 1950s is that this
historical tendency is precisely what was allowed
to happen in Queensland. But in a series of specific
instances an increased intentionality around the
relationship between buildings and the city, and
between the city as infrastructure and image,
defined the direction of the next generation's
lightly planned growth.

The three signature architectural works of
the 1950s Gold Coast were all projects of the
entrepreneur Stanley Korman, who sought to
import into the Gold Coast (a name that had his
explicit support) the amenities of the southern
cities of Sydney and Melbourne, and hence the

traffic of visitors north from those cooler climes.[10]
Langer's Lennon's Hotel (figs 5.10 and 5.11) had
reinvigorated the nineteenth-century Lennon brand
during its Brisbane hiatus (spanning from the
1940s to the 1970s) on a Broadbeach site, offering

5.11 Lennon's Broadbeach Hotel.

all that one would need on holiday – excepting its distance from the beach itself (requiring a decent hike across the sand from hotel to surf), and that it required a deliberate journey to the nearest bars and restaurants beyond its walls (Broadbeach then being undeveloped).[11] Katherine Rickard recalls its varied amenities: 'A five-storey accommodation wing containing sixty-eight double and forty single rooms sited amongst extensive recreation facilities, mostly outdoor, including a tennis court and bowling green, swimming pool, dance floor and bandstand, public bar, cocktail bar, restaurant and convention hall.'[12] Two Aboriginal artists – the brothers Yttca from across the state border in Tweed – contributed paintings and totems throughout the public interiors and outdoor zones. Lennon's won immediate professional acclaim, appearing on the cover of *Architecture and Arts* in 1957 and in *L'architecture d'aujourd'hui* and *Baumeister* in 1959 and 1960 respectively. But local journalist and historian Alexander McRobbie ultimately declared the hotel a 'white elephant', its evident sophistication as a venue and as a work of modern architecture and landscape undermined by Langer's stance that a hotel of such evident quality and amenity could only exist on a site in such relative isolation.[13] (It was, notably, one of two Lennon's hotels built on the Gold Coast at this precise moment, the other, attributed to Sydney-based Emil Sodersten at Kirra Beach (opposite the Surf Life Saving Club, fig. 5.12), more modest in scale and amenity.)

In Surfers Paradise and a short distance from the Surfers Paradise Hotel (off what is now Cavill Mall), Korman's Chevron Hotel (figs 5.13 and 5.14) broke ground in 1957 with a design by another Brisbane architect, David Bell. When its first stage (83 rooms) opened in Winter 1958, it proclaimed itself the pinnacle of luxury and sophistication – with all the amenities for which one could wish, the perfect location to enjoy the beach and the urban charms of Surfers Paradise, and decorative schemes that changed from room to room. (While it was intended as a Surfers Paradise Hilton, it would take the hotel chain another half century to claim a spot in what, by 2010, was a very different

5.12 Lennon's Kirra Hotel, Kirra Beach, 1958.

5.13 Chevron Hotel shops including a record bar, hairdresser and bottle shop, Surfers Paradise, 1960.

5.14 Chevron Hotel new accommodation wings and swimming pool, Surfers Paradise, 1958.

5.15 Kinkabool, the first-high rise building
in Surfers Paradise.

city.) Each room had a balcony and many enjoyed
ocean views. Korman's company had bought the
Surfers Paradise Hotel off the Cavill family shortly
after Jim Cavill's death. With one liquor licence
held by the Surfers Paradise Hotel and a second
secured for the Chevron, Korman effectively held
a monopoly on the city's drinking holes. A short
walk south but easy to see from a distance, the
ten-storey Kinkabool (originally called Poinciana
Place, fig. 5.15) on Hanlan Street in Surfers Paradise
was designed by the Brisbane firm of Ford, Hutton
and Newell, but was a product primarily of John
Morton's drawing board. The Gold Coast's first

'high-rise' residential complex (knocking Lennon's
claim as the South Coast's tallest building), it first
was occupied in 1961 and quickly followed by the
firm with Glenfalloch, in the Brisbane suburb of
New Farm.

All three of these projects would for one reason
or another suffer financial difficulty – not least, but
not only because of the nationwide credit squeeze
of 1960 that took a particularly public toll on Surfers
Paradise. Korman's company bought Kinkabool
before it was finished, with individual apartment
owners effectively becoming shareholders in
Stanhill Consolidated – which before the Building

Units Titles Act was passed in 1965 left 'owners' exposed to Korman's business fortunes. The marooned Lennon's closed its doors in 1987, having endured a slow and painful decline from its position as the height of sophistication in the 1950s and 1960s. The Chevron passed from one set of hands to another over the next decades. (Indeed, Korman's original project was demolished in 1989 in favour of a tower developed first by Theo Morris, then Ong Beng Seng, and finally the Raptis Group, with new buildings, embracing postmodernism as enthusiastically as Korman had welcomed its precedessor and designed by Christopher and Clark, and then DBI – successor to the Gold Coast office of Media Five.[14]) Jones has already underscored the importance of Korman's visions for the Chevron site for the city entire. Korman anticipated a moment in which professionals would commute between the Gold Coast and Sydney or Melbourne, and as such emphasised the city's accessibility by air when promoting his own properties.

In some important respects, these projects were landmark versions of a near ubiquitous architecture of tourism and travel – widespread in the city, and across the global tourism map. In some instances, they were the products of architectural design; in others, builder or owner-designed houses, motels and office blocks. These had been part of the South Coast landscape since its earliest days of colonial-era settlement. But rather than offering a setting for an escape from the pressures of central city Melbourne or the routine of farming life on the Darling Downs, these new projects purported, each in their own way, to be *the* place to vacation. Korman conceived of his projects as part of a system that extended from the bedroom and the pool to the airport and beyond, advocating the introduction of new services from the airport at Coolangatta (already running from 1947 to Sydney and Melbourne) to allow commuters to establish weekend homes up north and thereby positioning the Gold Coast as a hub in a modern east coast network of cities connected by air and investment rather than road or rail. These ambitions went well beyond the provision of plentiful rooms and entertainment and hence the motel scape of the old highway and shoreline. They established the

Gold Coast as the country's principal tourist city. Korman furthermore positioned the city as a testing ground for the most inventive new combinations of functions (combining a public house with a service station now seems particularly ill-advised), for floating the newest of (American) fashions, and for casting the vacation as an experience in comfort and convenience (the resort) rather than an opportunity to shed the conveniences of modern life with a spell at the beach-shack or camping ground.

The spectre of Miami dominates this decade, and the next. This American city had enjoyed its own boom in the wake of the 1930s, and like the developers Alfred Grant, Korman's contemporary, and Bruce Small, who followed in his wake, Korman saw no reason to imagine that the success of that city could not be replicated in Queensland's own south-east corner. Reflecting on the previous decade's efforts, Langer observed in 1959 that the 'virgin' dairy farmland that lay behind the narrow strip of beach-front real estate could be planned 'in a way which would provide many more of the coast's scarcest commodities – waterfront homesites.'[15] While we tend to favour the city's monuments to the good life in thinking about the architectural history of this city, the reshaping of its landscape to dramatically expand its real estate offerings and suburbanise its waterways is the most extensive and enduring architectural intervention in this decade. That the land behind the city was flood-prone was a technical challenge that could be overcome by deferring to Dutch canal building practices and American urbanism. The new estate overwrote the canals that had been dug to drain the Great Swamp around 1910, overlaying instances of pragmatic engineering with aspirational moments of urbanism and adapting a landscape infrastructure for the needs of property development.

The first of the city's new riverside estates dates to 1956 and was not a canal estate as such, even if it reclaimed land and treated a lucky few to water views and pontoon access to the water. Developed by Mick Ress of the Savoy Corporation, it effectively offered a new island in an elbow of the Nerang River where it met the Little Tallebudgera

5.16 View of a residence at 86–88 Savoy
Drive, Florida Gardens, 1959.

tenure in Florida Gardens. This estate was, at the time, the largest property development in the state of Queensland, even if it would quickly be dwarfed by its neighbours.

Following a background in the sale of pastoral estates, Alfred Grant entered the Gold Coast property development landscape in 1955, commencing work on two connected canal estates in 1957, with a layout designed by Langer (fig. 5.17). Grant had made fact-finding trips to the Hawaiian Islands and to Florida as the settings of major US coastal townships built on tourism. The estates of

5.18 View of Rio Vista and Miami Keys
under construction, c.1958.

Creek (now engineered beyond recognition) – all within Albert Shire, on land once subsumed by the so-called Great Swamp.[16] The Savoy project set the precedent for transforming pastoral land of varied quality into real estate. The estate was called Florida Gardens and followed no clear planning principle beyond the optimisation of land plots. The first house built upon it did little to proclaim it as the landmark development project history has shown it to have been: a single dwelling in mock Tudor style (fig. 5.16, still standing) on Savoy Drive was the first dwelling built there, or rather moved there in 1959, since it had begun life at Surfers Paradise some years earlier before taking up its

Rio Vista and Miami Keys in the area now called Broadbeach Waters were laid out on perpendicular main axes flanking Florida Gardens, with the disposition of houses following the principles first tested in the industry town of Radburn, New Jersey, and given their most famous expression in the Los Angeles community of Baldwin Hills Village (1941). As Ian Sinnamon once put it, Langer traded 'blue for green' in his adaptation of the Radburn planning principle for neighbourhoods built around waterways (fig. 5.18).[17] While the Village Green of Baldwin Hills (for instance) turned houses away from the street so they addressed their neighbours over a common park, Langer had

5.17 View of Rio Vista and Miami Keys
under construction, c.1958.

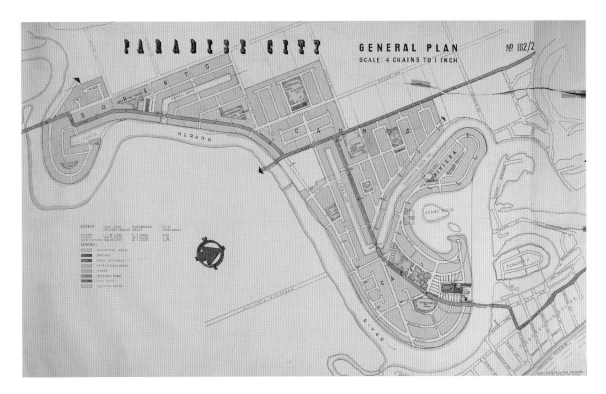

5.19 Paradise City, 1959.

the houses of Rio Vista and Miami Keys interact over the canals, suggesting a new community maintained over water.

Bruce Small's Paradise City (fig. 5.19) followed these first canal estates as though he himself had thought of the idea – and it was, like the projects before it, laid out on Langer's drawing board. Although the architect gained national, even international attention for his modernist architectural designs in Queensland on the basis of his houses and civic amenities, it was with his designs for new estates and suburbs that Langer made an enduring contribution to the form and organisation of this city. His scheme for Paradise City is broken into four zones, only one of which was realised as proposed: Sorrento, Cannes, Capri and Riviera. Small's allusions were not particularly subtle. Touted as Queensland's first planned city, it included plots of land for new homes, as well as

sporting facilities, recreation grounds, a bathers' beach, a supermarket and shops at walking distance from any home, churches (gathered together on a single block, backs to each other) and a civic centre (facing across the Nerang River on to Paradise Island). A small number of new canals would increase the number of properties with a water frontage, and a small boat harbour would allow residents to moor their vessels close to home. Across the river sat Grant's Rio Vista development – another Langer project, but not a Small endeavour – and which is in the plan presented as blank, unlike the pre-existing street grid of Surfers Paradise to the east. A town planning board would review the design of individual houses to ensure a consistent architectural vocabulary.

Like Korman before him, Small promoted the city alongside his own developments, framing it as the ideal location both for families and for those who, like him, sought warmer climes for their retirement years. (Small's own Gold Coast years had begun when he was in his sixties.) His projects include the Isle of Capri, the only realised part of the Paradise City scheme, as well as Sorrento, Benowa (where his own vast house was built) and Cypress Gardens. He did so first as a developer, then as a developer-mayor-alderman, being elected to office in 1967 (1967–73; 1976–78) with the slogan 'Think Big, Vote Small'. Although the legend locates Small's enthusiasm for canal estates with his own visit to Miami in 1958, he was doing little more than following in the footsteps of Grant, whose projects were earlier, more extensive and more rationally planned. That said, Small's ambitions were clearly and persuasively stated, not just for Paradise City, but for the Gold Coast as a whole: 'Where, once, milch cows browsed knee-deep in lush meadows, a vast sweep of land, river locked, has been garden-landscaped on a massive scale to bring a new design of gracious living to those who seek a "place in Paradise".' His language complements Langer's design like the thick cream of post-war affluence observed by Robin Boyd (quoted at the start of this book). No line captures it better than the final passage in the Paradise City marketing: 'A dream city? Yes, as dreamy as the slumberous sheets of foam that endlessly turn on the nearby beaches. Here, in their own sub-tropical haven, the citizens of Paradise City may live – and enjoy – a life as rich in early blessings as Man and Nature could devise.'[18]

An eight-day carnival supported by the Gold Coast Chamber of Commerce marked the opening of the Isle of Capri. More than 200 interstate guests, capable of peddling influence, were brought to the city and given the full, spectacular treatment, with receptions, fashion parades, and a heavily mediated introduction to the domestic, civil and religious life of this new city. The task was to sell the city by marketing directly to those figures who could shape the city's reception elsewhere, investing heavily in the Gold Coast as an idea that

could be marketed and sold. But neither Small's hyperbole nor his ambition were matched by the realised development. As Jones' has most surgically assessed it, 'Paradise City today is really just a slice of suburbia ... '[19]

In their earliest phases, the canal estates opened up an affordable stream of real estate, and the houses built on the edges of the Nerang tended to be ubiquitous, off-the-plan homes that had been realised *en masse* and suddenly. The innovation of the estates, beyond their solution of myriad technical issues, lay with the adaptation of land-based urban planning for the waterways. In a history distinguished for its relative invisibility, a layer overwritten for the same reasons as brought it into being, these estates are the last monumental vestiges of the modern adventure on which the South Coast embarked after the Second World War. They were also a confronting development for the country's architectural critics at the end of the decade. Not only was this small city built on sun, surf and sand, but it had established the terms for its own longevity, reclaiming and constructing without restraint alongside river, creek and sea. It is telling that many of the fine modern works of the post-war years were subsequently overwritten through the need for better returns and the extraordinary demand that would accrue to the sea-side plots on which they once sat. By the end of the 1950s, the Gold Coast, as it had become, sat between an aspiring culture of city building and a perplexed architectural culture, and critics, architects and planners were caught between expressing curiosity and disdain. Within their analysis and judgments emerged the question of what to do next; and of the extent to which architects and town planners should act in response to this sudden critical attention upon a city that had seemed to spring up out nowhere. In this, the pages of *Architecture in Australia* once more offer a vital gauge of the city's problems and possibilities, and this just a year after Eddie Hayes penned his own reflections. To 1959 ...

6 City of Types

In the year following the publication of Eddie Hayes's observations on the nature of practising architecture on the Gold Coast, the town received

OURNAL OF THE ROYAL AUSTRALIAN INSTITUTE OF ARCHITECTS

6.1 Cover of the *Gold Coast* issue of *Architecture in Australia*, 1959.

its charter. By the end of 1959 it would be proclaimed the City of Gold Coast. In its first issue of that year, the RAIA journal, *Architecture in Australia* (*AA*, fig. 6.1), once again turned to the nature of what was in that moment a city in the making, and to the problems and potential of architecture, town planning and professional architectural practice in that setting. This time, though, the journal dedicated the entire issue to a topic Hayes had given just a single page in 1958. The monographic Gold Coast issue remains one of the most serious assessments of the city's architecture published to date, looking with scepticism to architecture's relation to such industrial processes as tourism and real estate development. It attends, as well, to the scale of city and landscape – where both were being reconfigured as a result of architectural interventions in the fabric of this city-region, which it clearly understood not as a Gold Coast strictly defined, but as a municipality encroaching systematically on the territory and culture of its neighbours. In becoming the Australian capital of recreation, the Gold Coast posed a set of unprecedented problems to the country's architectural culture. *AA* thus cast a critical eye with a view towards a better future. The problems were by no means new, but in their relative intensity they were difficult to ignore.

Importantly, the city had posed the question of the profession's responsibility for a city in which architects had either involved themselves with

6.2 Offices of Cavill Real Estate diagonally
opposite the Chevron Hotel, Elkhorn
Avenue, Surfers Paradise, *c*.1958.

a light touch (if at all) or allowed their talents to
wholeheartedly serve as instruments of profitability
to the exclusion of all other considerations. In this,
any architect who was involved in this city was one
way or another compromised.

The journal reflected back the national
architectural culture Australia's cultural touchiness
to the Gold Coast's troubling idiosyncrasies: 'When
sensitive individuals', reads one of four editorial
essays, 'begin to speak of lovely coastlines still
unspoilt by man and begin to fear that development
may equal despoliation, one indeed must wonder
about the condition of our civilisation. The
present regional picture of the Gold Coast seems
to underline all those anxieties and fears.' It goes
on: 'Without hesitation and with much splendid

foresight [the Constituted Authority] should tackle
and solve the burning problems of roadways,
townscapes, localities, waterways and parks: the

6.3 View towards Surfers Paradise.

6.4 Silver Sands, Surfers Paradise.

gold of the Coast otherwise will turn to dross in less than a generation's time.'[1] This turned out to be no isolated expression of reticence. For many years, the relation between individual architectural achievements and their cumulative import for the entire city were at the forefront of Australia's reception of Gold Coast architecture.

The articles survey the problem of this city while declaring lines of enquiry for the architectural community as it moved into the 1960s. H. J. (John) Hitch positions the Gold Coast in the tradition of the spa and seaside resort towns, starting from British precedents and moving to their American uptake. Southport began its recreational life in

conversation with the seaside towns of England, but it ended with an exchange with the resort towns of Florida. The city 'measures up' to its famous British precedents only to the extent that there are parts of the hinterland that '*have never been fully and imaginatively commercialised by the business community of the coast as a mighty visual back drop to hotels or restaurants*.'[2] As a whole, it had fallen between the attentions of local and state governments, with no single body ensuring that the demands of a growing permanent population will be met by the city in which it lives. Hitch isolates those sites capable of sustaining strategic densification and increased pedestrianisation as the key to the city's future, offering his own impression (fig. 6.5) of how the Gold Coast could accommodate a modern civic centre. But, he concludes: 'The easy boom is over – and has left virtually nothing to posterity.'[3]

Elsewhere in this issue Peter Newell (a Queenslander among Victorians and Sydneysiders) makes his own assessment of how the Gold Coast has stood up to its history. In 'Umbigumbi to the Gold Coast' he recalls the phases of development explored earlier in this book and summarised by Hayes in 1958. These phases take the form, for him, in the khaki of explorers and settlers; the advent of building regulations; the arrival of asbestos cement and casual construction; and 'consolidation' – the

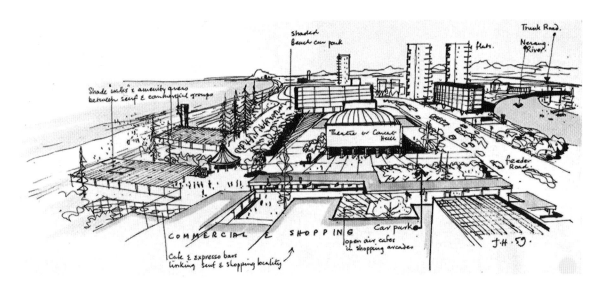

6.5 Scheme for a Gold Coast Civic Centre.
Drawing by John Hitch in the *Gold Coast*
issue of *Architecture in Australia*, 1959.

problem of the present. He defers to the common points of concern: the expense of waterfront land, the high-rise towers, the questionable progress of the canal estates and the Americanisation they herald, and the destruction of the city's natural assets in the name of real estate development. 'The Tudor, Baronial and Romanesque houses still appear, looking more incongruous than ever.'[4] With echoes of Hayes's conclusions he asks, 'Can we, as architects and town planners, create a gay, vital, but disciplined and enlightened environment for the Gold Coast – or will this playground degenerate into another CONEY ISLAND?'[5]

Ostensibly offering a case for 'An Ideal Holiday Resort on the Gold Coast', Milo Dunphy turns to this problem, considering the impact of the city's suburban growth on a key visual mechanism: the dramatic contrasts between lush nature and intense urbanism that gives the Coast its 'symbolic identity'. He argues that 'towns such as Surfers' Paradise are vital emergents in a luxuriant swamp. The vitality of the vision depends largely upon the emphasis provided by the verdant context.'[6] Dunphy asserts that the future importance of the Gold Coast as a holiday resort would rest on the city's capacity to protect its greenbelt, by which he also means its capacity to protect the sudden contrasts from bush to city that register not with the pedestrian, but with the motorist (fig. 6.6).

Elsewhere in the issue, (László) Peter Kollar made his own assessment known: the 'grave mistakes that abound on the Gold Coast from a regional planning point of view must be clear to anybody looking upon the spectacle from unbiased eyes.'[7] But these are only mistakes if one assumes that the maturity of a new city can be planned meticulously from its foundations, and if one allows that the kind of unexpected growth as sustained by the Gold Coast in the decades leading up to Queensland's centennial year of 1959 (and continuing beyond) could be absorbed effortlessly into forward thinking of an exceptional prescience. Outlining what he calls the 'first major step towards serious urban planning', Kollar makes the case for what eventually transpired in the form of the M1, namely a major motorway running from New South Wales to Brisbane but never touching the city, being fed by minor arterials connecting the pockets of urban density to the city's infrastructure. This solution, he argues, must be one of three elements of an integrated solution involving, too, the waterways and protection of greenbelts (echoing Dunphy). The effect would be to pull traffic out of the city as it stands, and to free up the Pacific Highway (now the Gold Coast Highway) for local traffic, rather than routing interstate traffic through the Coast's strained two-lane roadways. Langer's Lennon's Hotel is, in this proposal, the warning in perpetuity (even within five years of its completion): its relationship to its surroundings 'unfortunate from the start', its mass never reconciled either with the topography or the sparse construction in its vicinity.[8] He argues that the Gold Coast, too, needed to start operating as a system of networks and nodes, demanding that nature, street systems and urban pockets be interrelated to overcome the impasse of the present.

An article by Karl Langer explains the sources and technical challenges involved in the first of the canal estates introduced in the previous chapter, already indicating the future proliferation in this planning type by announcing the purchase of 'many hundreds of acres adjacent to Miami Keys and Rio Vista ... for similar development.'[9] The editors, however, eye these developments with barely concealed derision, dedicating an entire editorial segment to their reservations.[10]

Presentations of David Bell's design for the Chevron Hotel, the Mermaid Beach Car-a-Park Motel (Hayes and Scott), the Methodist Church in Southport (Douglas and Barnes) and the refurnished dining room of the Surfers Paradise Hotel (Bligh,

6.6 Lush nature vs intense urbanism. Sketch by Milo Dunphy in the *Gold Coast* issue of *Architecture in Australia*, 1959.

6.7 Tiki Village as seen from the Nerang
River, Surfers Paradise, 1968.

Jessop, Bretnall and Partners in a Trewern building)
sit alongside three speculative towers for Surfers
Paradise: a reprise of the Torbreck Home Units
(Job and Froud – a variation of the units illustrated
in Chapter 5), a stout tower by Ford, Hutton and
Newell, and another Douglas and Barnes design,
for the Taj Surfers Paradise. While these name the
critics' choice of the best work done in the most
recent years, they also endorse a clear strain of
the more projective signals of the future and their
combined strategies of pedestrian life and high
density living. The issue closes with articles by
Marjorie St Henry (an alderman of the Gold Coast
Town Council, as it was at the time of the issue's
publication); C. A. (Gus) Kelly (Chief Secretary of
the Minister in Charge of Tourist Activities) on the
prospects of northern New South Wales to extend
the Gold Coast's fortunes on its own terms; and J. H.
Shaw on technical issues around land reclamation
and subdivisional planning – all with an eye on
those current planning problems that have a clear
importance to the region's future.[11]

First writing in the pages of *The Age* in 1957,
Robin Boyd had made his definitive statements
on the Gold Coast in *The Australian Ugliness*. He
had therein called Surfers Paradise a 'poor man's
Miami',[12] pointing to its abundance of regrettable
taste and the concomitant relaxation of the culture
the produced it – the curious mix of Australian
society and American style that he thought to
demonstrate in its extremity those tendencies to
which all Australia would in time become subject.

Culturally speaking, the scorn and derision it sustained was inevitably tempered with an anxiety over where and how its symptoms might normalise elsewhere, a concern best expressed in Boyd's invocation of the skin-deep ugliness he saw covering the cities of his country. As noted at the outset of this present work, the editors of *AA* in 1959 expressed their disbelief that 'people can be so completely oblivious of the shortcomings and coarseness of their surroundings.' The causes rest with the special kind of environmental apathy that accompanies the 'respectable family from the south' on their northern holidays. All that one would normally insist upon was here absent, undermined by chaos and lack of vision. The editors declare their intentions to properly diagnose the former, and offer something for the latter. To recall the last line of the opening editorial: 'It may be too late for the Gold Coast though not elsewhere.'[13]

A concluding editorial, consequently, concerns 'The Architecture': a fitting relegation of architecture *as such* behind the mechanics of civic management and regional planning, where architecture's stakes in the city were being defined. 'Gold Coast architecture, in the strict sense of the word, is practically non-existent. The part architects played in creating this bubbling ribbon is infinitesimal.'[14] The problems of the Gold Coast, they go on to assert, confront architecture's responsibilities towards the city as any gesture 'good or bad that permanently marks the landscape.' In this sense, the problem of the Gold Coast is an architectural problem demanding an expanded sense of architecture's location and effects.

This issue of *AA* captured the Gold Coast in its process of becoming *the* Gold Coast: the proliferation of such building types as the themed bar and the motel, the accommodation in city structures of the motorcar, the invitation to experiment in form and expression in the provision of an infrastructure for tourism. It acknowledged, too, the accommodation both within the city limits and beyond of buildings and neighbourhoods that resolved new combinations of function and reconciled, as Boyd had astutely observed, the most progressive American responses to the individual

mobility and freedom afforded by the family car and to the boom experienced by a generation that had fought in Europe and the Pacific and were now enjoying the profits of peace. That these had been a success for the Gold Coast in the decade after it had shrugged off the mantle of the mere 'South' Coast was duly noted. The concern expressed in these pages, however, lay with the possibility of being able to distinguish 'the weed from the precious shoot' in embedding all of the qualities that made the Gold Coast perfect for a holiday away from the quotidian into the workings of a city and the cultural demands made of both architecture and its citizenry. And the Gold Coast of 1959? The Institute of Architects claims the final word: 'It is now an automated holiday production line mixed haphazardly with the remnants of the past of not so long ago.'[15]

Casting forward fifteen years: the most prominent building on the Surfers Paradise foreshore was designed by the Sydney-based architects and planners Clarke, Gazzard and Partners. The distinctive Focus tower (fig. 6.8), circular in plan, would monitor the northern end of Surfers Paradise from 1974 to the present day. (The architects had consulted on the landmark Sydney building Australia Square, designed by Harry Seidler in collaboration with the Italian engineer Pier Luigi Nervi, 1961 and 1967 – which Focus clearly references.) Standing near to 100 metres in height, more than 30 levels, it has gradually been overtaken by later generations of tall buildings. But even today its profile is a striking monument to the city's ambitions in the 1970s. Focus predicated a boom period of development including low, medium and high density building types and resulting, therefore, in a substantial increase in the city's high-rise building stock. This boom responded in part to the factors that had seen the Gold Coast's growth since the late 1950s. It also responded to a new legislative development under the State government of Joh Bjelke-Petersen to abolish death duties for Queensland residents. While this was a cynical attempt to draw wealth north from Victoria and New South Wales, it had a major impact on the Gold Coast's building economy as individuals contemplating where to spend their retirement

6.8 Demolition on Surfers Paradise, with a
view on Focus.

began decisively voting for the sun. This turned the
Gold Coast into a real estate investment haven of
sorts for a generation tempted both by the agreeable
climate and by the prospect of retaining their assets
for family upon their demise.

Michael Jones summarises the numbers
involved. From 1963 to 1970, there had been 6,220
approvals for flats and apartments, 'mainly low-
rise'. From 1970 to 1977, there were 8,369, a slight
increase over the previous seven-year period. In the
next two years, another 6,782 approvals were grants,
then 10,885 from 1981–83. 'There were 17,627 flats,
mainly high-rise, approved from 1978 to 1983 [the

6.9 Aerial view of Surfers Paradise,
1980s.

first five years after the abolition in Queensland of death duties], a number that exceeded the 14,859 flats approved between 1963 and 1977.'[16] Over the course of the 1970s, the intersection of public and private interests was beginning to register as a tension in the city's most heavily built up zones, and as Jones elsewhere observes, the relationship between real estate development and the natural resource of the beach became a key question in public debate around the urban impact of private interests – embodied in the widely cited problem of the shadows cast over the beach by the city's new tall buildings.[17]

Indeed, in the five years following 1977, Surfers Paradise saw built nearly fifty new towers exceeding the height of the city's original ten-storey high-rise, Kinkabool. These extended, though, tendencies already cemented in the city by a series of prominent firms and projects. Two towers by

Emery Nemes – famous as consultant architect to Westfield – remain significant moments of mid-century Surfers Paradise modernism: The Sands (on the Esplanade, 1964–66), a slick nod to Miami and Honolulu; and Paradise Towers (on the Gold Coast Highway, 1965–66), an off-the-plan speculative project with a distinctive atrium core, ground-floor shopping arcade and generous individual balconies, which followed Kinkabool as the city's second prominent high-rise building. The Melbourne firm of Buchan, Laird and Bawden likewise had a strong presence on the Gold Coast from the 1960s onwards and under Bill Heather established a local office in 1972. Extending lessons derived from the firm's well-established relationships with American architects, the Buchan Laird and Bawden towers offered investors economically planned and carefully programmed resort towers in close proximity to the water:

6.10 The Esplanade (and Iluka) and Cavill Avenue, Surfers Paradise, c.1975.

Suntower (completed 1968), the Shore (1969–70), Iluka (fig. 6.10, completed 1971, demolished) and the Chateau (1971–72). The vocabulary does not vary significantly from one project to the next, but they grew taller with time.[18]

Although the developments of the 1950s and 1960s had caught the city off-guard, to an extent, the work of the 1970s responded to a loose set of development guidelines in the form of a strategic plan that operated at the level of municipal zoning and service provision while leaving architects and developers largely undisturbed in their realisation of individual buildings. The Gold Coast had doubled its population over the course of the 1960s, demanding a more thoughtful outlook for the continued growth its managers anticipated. What would a mature city on the Gold Coast require? Where might its services expand? What might need formal protection? These were the questions posed to Clarke, Gazzard in the mid-1960s in their briefing to prepare the city's first strategic plan. In this enterprise, the figure of Bruce Small looms large. Citizens had indeed 'thought big' in supporting his real estate development enterprises over the previous decade. Small understood that the city's growth was not about to abate, and that a system encouraging enterprise while planning for the future would secure the city's long-term prospects. Adopted in March 1969, the *Gold Coast Urban Region: Strategic Plan 1970–1990* took the criticisms that had been levelled at the Gold Coast in the 1959 issue of *AA*, considered its trajectory across the subsequent decade, and sought to anticipate the needs of the city as a complex urban management problem that would inevitably play out over the next two decades. That they would immediately thereafter realise the Focus tower in Surfers Paradise is an indication of their proximity to the city's concerns, and offers an immediate, interior response to the possibilities of the *Strategic Plan*.

The preamble to the report identified a number of needs that had been provoked by the 'explosive' growth to which the Gold Coast had been subject since the end of the Second World War. Trading the diagnoses published in 1959 for action, they described the major arterial roads

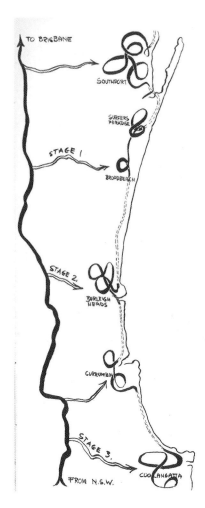

6.11 L. Peter Kollar, Ribbon and Feeder Roads, in *Architecture in Australia*, 1959.

the city would need, arguing for well-planned street systems within the precincts defined by those roads (fig. 6.11). They noted the need for regulated open spaces, including nature reserves at varying levels of government protection from national parks to local parks. The plan made the case for water and sewerage systems that anticipated growth rather than responding to immediate demands. They accommodated flood mitigation planning, including drainage schemes and erosion controls. They made

6.12 View of the Pacific Highway, Surfers Paradise, c.1965.

GOLD COAST URBAN HERITAGE & CHARACTER STUDY

'God I love this place,
some of these buildings are twenty years old'
Steve Martin, LA Story.

Allom Lovell Marquis-Kyle • Henshall Hansen Associates • Context • HJM • Staddon Consulting

6.13 Cover of the *Gold Coast Urban Heritage & Character Study* (1997).

allowance for special zones to be set aside for schools at all levels, from primary schools to advanced technical institutes (including the site now named the Health and Knowledge Precinct, in Parklands), all in response to population projections. They argued for a 'regional system of new and/or extended public airports' and facilities for private aircraft. A full generation before the amalgamation with Albert Shire, they predicated the need for a 'new administration for the Gold Coast City Council' and for a cultural centre, either as part of the projected establishment of a university or technical training college, or as part of the new civic centre. And they observed the need for a 'future commercial centre which can grow in an orderly manner and which will

be capable of serving the whole region.' These recommendations served the aim of introducing controls into private land development in order to provide urban services fundamental to the city's ability to act as such, and to accommodate further growth.

While the *Strategic Plan* did not dictate the immediate future of the Gold Coast, it described a way beyond the simple diagnosis of its problems by a generation of critics who had found it wanting. The ongoing absence of building controls was for some a boon, allowing architects and developers to quickly exploit opportunities to build; while for others it was an enduring sign of the city's lack of maturity. In moving through the 1970s and 1980s, however, the municipality consolidated the city's infrastructure along lines that had been sketched out by Clarke, Gazzard and Partners, even if all that was projected in their image of the city's future would not eventuate as they had anticipated it might.

These decades saw the construction of major shopping precincts in Southport (Scarborough Fair, now Australia Fair) and Broadbeach (Pacific Fair), each heralding a monumental postmodernism in their respective settings. The casino that opened as Jupiter's in 1985, on Broadbeach Island, was in fact part of Albert Shire, but for the first decade the two municipalities enjoyed its impact on their respective economies. This project is noteworthy for the strength of the Gold Coast's ambitions to have Queensland's second casino licence be awarded to a project in the city (or its vicinity), with over three quarters of the twenty tenders submitted state-wide seeking the licence for a site in the Gold Coast or Albert Shire. The list of unsuccessful Gold Coast sites recorded in the Rider-Hunt Development Report (July 1981) indicates the varied ways in which the city could have been drawn at this time: a proposal by Golden Nugget for a casino at the Main Beach Spit, two projects around the site of the Chevron Hotel, two in downtown Surfers Paradise, another at Palm Beach, another still at the Surfers Paradise International Raceway in Bundall (with a second in Slayter Avenue, Bundall) and, significantly, greenfield developments at Carrara and Robina (the latter, perhaps the most prophetic in its complexity, involving a design proposal by the Canadian architect Moshe Safdie).[19] The successful project had been proposed by Jennings Industries and was realised to the design of Buchan Laird and Bawden, offering on its Broadbeach site a new anchor for a second phase of high density, high-rise development that would accelerate rapidly from the 1990s onwards.

While the era of Korman and Small had ensured the coincidence of real estate development and spectacular events, the establishment of a series of theme parks and integrated resorts across the 1980s likewise shaped the flow of tourists and their dollars through the city. Established in 1970 by Keith Williams, Sea World was the model for such later theme parks as Movie World, White Water World, and Dream World, all built along the northern corridor bifurcated by the M1. The idea of travelling

to resorts within the Gold Coast that required no further interaction with the city was, too, thoroughly explored in such ventures of the late 1980s as the Marina Mirage (and later Sport Mirage) on the Southport Spit. The Melbourne-trained architect Desmond Brooks deserves particular mention in this context for his importance to the scale change of the complexes built to satisfy all the demands of a family on holiday. Returning to Australia from the United States via Hawaii in 1982, he established a branch of the Pan-Pacific, Honolulu-based firm of Media Five. Under its aegis, Brooks designed the Marina developments, as well as the Gold Coast International Hotel (now QT). His successor firm, DBI Design, has gone on to dominate the city's high rise designs (alongside developer-architects Sunland) in the boom periods in which the city's postmodern hotels and first integrated resorts were built and, much more recently, in which those

6.14 **Gold Coast Highway looking south,**
*c.*1970.

towers competing with an international cohort of record-setting heights were, one after the other, declared open.

While the integrated record had a clear precedent in Langer's design for Lennon's Broadbeach, the sheer volume, extent and variety of tourist complexes realised in the last four decades speaks to the city's new standing among a network of Asia-Pacific recreational sites – no longer just a playground for Australians in need of a holiday, but a city capturing moments in the global movement of tourists.

The Gold Coast's internationalisation, its then recent merger with Albert Shire, and the growing sense of its need to assert a specific identity shaped by its history underpinned the project to conduct the *Gold Coast Urban Heritage and Character Study* that was published in 1997.[20] While the Clarke, Gazzard *Strategic Plan* had sought to help the Gold Coast act like a city, the *Urban Heritage and Character Study* set out to help the city act like the Gold Coast. A broad-based review of the city's social, urban, cultural and architectural history, the study sought to distil values from its multifarious pasts, augmented by input by local residents, that could inform the future of the city and its suburbs in order to ensure their connection with a sense of identity. What, it asked, had the Gold Coast been before the chaos of its internationalisation? What acts and values had defined the city *as* the Gold Coast? How might this heritage inform the city's future directions? For all that it might be problematic as an attempt to regulate the Gold Coast's architecture and urbanism and shape its

nascent cultural programme, the *Urban Heritage and Character Study* offered the first major assessment of these matters without needing to work through a defence of the city's legitimacy. The result was an overcorrection that underpinned increased aesthetic and environmental controls based on a dubious 'sense of place'.

Writing on architectural and urban history therein, Philip Goad demonstrated the superfluity of specific architectural works by limiting his analysis to those aspects of urban morphology (beach, highway, canal estate, suburb, hinterland) and to those building types (holiday house/unit, motel, residential tower, theme park, shopping mall) that shaped the city's character.[21] As such, he productively reverted to the terms of the 1959 analysis, while offering a typological history of the post-war city that eclipsed all that preceded.

Among numerous references to American precedents and to the clear and cultivated parallels between the Gold Coast and Miami, Langer's Lennon's Hotel is the only discrete work of Gold Coast architecture mentioned by Goad, having been notable for its demolition a decade earlier. Despite its plea for an open approach to the next chapter in the city's history, the effect of this history has been to reinforce among architects and planners a view that the authentic contemporary city must measure itself against the moment when it first self-consciously became a city: the late 1950s, when it was rejected by the architectural profession for its crass manifestation of an Austerica that had, in the decades since and just as feared, secured a place in Australia's urban culture everywhere.

7 Vegas in Paradise

The efforts made from the end of the 1950s to assess the Gold Coast as a city reflected three interrelated conditions. First, the realised city seemed to have appeared rapidly and without structure from the series of townships on which its early tourism industry had built, which rendered it both a curiosity for architects and town planners – and a problem. For if the South Coast had transmogrified so hastily into the Gold Coast, then no city, no township, was safe from the forces that had led to the advent of Surfers Paradise. Second, the Gold Coast embodied the problem of the twentieth-century city before Canberra, which had hitherto been Australia's sole beacon of modern urbanism (and which had not yet moved significantly beyond the Griffin plan): to what references and tactics would Australian urbanism defer in those cities unburdened with a nineteenth-century core? Did the nonchalantly conceived Gold Coast – rather than the highly intentioned scheme for Canberra – reflect the aspirations and values of Australian city life? And finally, by extension, it became clear that Australia's encounter with American culture in the Pacific War had invited a conversation between sun-belt towns that had enjoyed similar conditions across the middle decades of the twentieth century, such as Miami, Los Angeles and Honolulu – and, less directly, Mediterranean leisure towns. Initially, Miami offered the most direct point of reference between continents – thanks to the proliferation of canal estates along the Nerang River and the art deco vocabulary used to inform the first civic buildings in both Southport and Surfers Paradise. And as the gambling town of Las Vegas acquired international fame in the 1950s, achieving an iconic status built on the tourist dollar, its renowned success reinforced those values on which the Gold Coast itself was self-consciously drawing.

This comparison was legitimised within architectural and cultural circles with the publication of *Learning from Las Vegas*, by Robert Venturi, Denise Scott-Brown and Steven Izenour, in 1972 – its photography and 'kitschiness' appealing to a postmodern public eager to reconsider the bases of thinking around the city and architecture, pondering the dual rise of the motorcar and consumerism and their impact on the city.[1] The book positioned Las Vegas as the American city *par excellence*, simultaneously casting it as both a model and an exception – a status the Gold Coast had already come to share, in its own way and for a different set of observers. Its authors borrowed their analysis of the desert city from documentary photography and cinematography, rallying their methods behind conceptual gains that had been put into play in architectural theory in the eighteenth and nineteenth centuries in appreciating the coherence of the city view. Of course, for participants in Yale's 1968 Las Vegas Research Studio, which the book records, it was a curiosity:

they had a job to do, while revelling in the bad taste of it all. But by now, cultured individuals like architects, town planners and artists had the tools to allow them to travel ironically to Las Vegas, as did Venturi, Scott Brown, Izenour and their students from the Yale School of Art and Architecture. Las Vegas was claimed as a new kind of subject for a new generation of studies that opened out on to new kinds of concerns for architectural criticism. The post-modern city was no longer (necessarily) where things would go terribly wrong for architecture, culture and planning.

The first systematic test of the importance of Las Vegas – and *Learning from Las Vegas* – for the Australian city coincided with the years in which the Gold Coast was settling into the image suggested by the developments of the 1960s. It is an interesting case both as an episode in the treatment of the Gold Coast as a subject of architectural criticism *and* as a chapter (little appreciated, until very recently) in the history of Australian postmodernism.

Its origins are as unexpected as they are intrinsic to the account, located as they are with the preoccupations of a group of young architects and teachers who joined Neville Quarry in Lae at the Papua New Guinea Institute of Technology to establish a school of architecture in this newly independent country. Quarry predominantly drew staff from his own former students and colleagues at the University of Melbourne, and their circles. Conditions were highly favourable to faculty prepared to commit to two or four-year contracts. From Melbourne, he attracted Ken Costigan (who would dedicate decades to the country as an architect and educator), Tony Styant-Browne (with his wife, Julie Jame, who had studied architecture at the University of Melbourne and graphic design and fine art at RMIT) and Adrian Boddy; from Sydney, Janet Grey; and from Brisbane, Gordon Holden – all a decade or more his junior, and all committed to the idea of teaching architecture to a first generation of nation-builders (the first two graduates gaining their diplomas in 1974). John Gollings was an occasional presence, too, although early on trading architecture for photography. Malcolm (Mal) Horner was a graduate of the City College of New York and

taught planning. Closer to Quarry's own age were Stan Barker, another Melbourne alumnus; Arthur Thomas, a Japanese Englishman with colonial public works experience; and Dimitri Perno (from Queensland's Sunshine Coast, who would later work in Samoa.[2]

The school was open to experimentation in pedagogy and research, and in many respects the faculty seized upon Lae as a liberating experience, revelling in the adventure, but dedicated, too, to the task of introducing the architecture profession to a new territory.

Styant-Browne bought his copy of *Learning from Las Vegas* at Jervis Manton in Melbourne in 1972 before commencing his two-year tenure in Lae. In America, Scott Brown and Izenour, in particular, had continued to apply the methodological gains of *Learning from Las Vegas* to analyse other American cities. Melbourne architect Corbett Lyon recalls following a studio in graduate school at the University of Pennsylvania where Izenour led a study of Atlantic City on these terms, one of a number of iterations to which the cinematic, windscreen view had been elsewhere applied.[3] Quite independent of this immediate afterlife to the Las Vegas project, Styant-Browne could clearly see the application of their approach to the Gold Coast, and Surfers Paradise in particular, responding to Boyd's critique and a prevailing sense that this town offered the kind of bad taste townscape that had fed the Yale students' experience in Las Vegas. Boyd's Austerica appealed to those of a younger generation who had followed the emergence of pop in the fine and applied arts and the culture of the beat generation – much of which being known less through any first-hand experience than through novels, films, essays, music and magazines.

Styant-Browne's father, Geoffrey Styant-Browne, had been one of the culprits of the Austericanism of the Gold Coast that would become an object of his son's analysis a generation later, with a number of neon-bordered gas stations, Californian-inspired motels and private houses to his name – including a house for the proprietors of the El Rancho BBQ, Dennis and Norma Dalton. The family had lived on the Coast during the younger Styant-Browne's

7.1 Round House (Styant-Browne residence, architect
Geoffrey Styant-Browne), Surfers Paradise.

7.2 Daw's Shell Petrol Station (architect
Geoffrey Styant-Browne), Surfers Paradise.

7.3 & 7.4 John Gollings, Surfers Paradise Boulevard looking south from The Shore at Night, Surfers Paradise, 1974/2013.

formative years, and he was familiar with the impoverished, yet peppy, signage and tacky *architecture parlante* of the small city's tourist strip of the years flanking 1960. Like Las Vegas, the Gold Coast was unburdened by a nineteenth-century plan. It was a strip, orientated from its urban-scale inception towards the needs of the motorist, who in this case was likely arriving to the Gold Coast along the main highway connecting nearby Brisbane

to Sydney. It was not Vegas – any more than it was Los Angeles or Miami Beach – but it was the closest thing available to test out the way that Venturi, Scott Brown, Izenour, and their students had undertaken their assessment of the contemporary, car-orientated city. If the American treatment of Las Vegas seemed worthy of emulation, it was on several bases. Both cities had grown from nothing on the basis of economies derived from pleasure and the

illicit. Both had condensed, in a comparatively extreme urban expression, values that had become widespread in their respective cultures – while both being widely regarded as cities devoid of civilised life. Both, furthermore, describe a moment of victory for popular culture over high culture.

Together with Gollings (from Melbourne) and Horner (from Lae), Styant-Browne and Jame (also Lae-based) planned a two-week vacation in January

1974 in which the team researched, strategised and undertook a study of Surfers Paradise in particular and the Gold Coast more generally in the mode of the Yale Las Vegas project. Their work sought to validate a (the) postmodern Australian city and its architecture, both of which were exhibiting the same tendencies as the strip city captured in *Learning from Las Vegas*, and to do so by turning the analytical tools employed by the Las Vegas Research Studio upon Surfers. The Papua New Guinea contingent travelled the 1,500 miles by air and the Gollings family drove 1,000 miles from Melbourne – the car

quickly converted to those same purposes to which the Yale students had turned their complimentary rental car five years earlier, with Gollings trading a bonnet-mounted camera for the more casual arrangement of sitting, himself, on the bonnet to shoot with a Widelux F6.[4]

Their images are on occasion rather more moody than the starkly lit Las Vegas photographs. The weather was against them (with major flood events occurring across Queensland's south-east corner that month), but between rain squalls and over a two-week period, Gollings, Styant-Browne, Jame

7.5 & 7.6 John Gollings, Florida Gardens Estate, Broadbeach, 1974/2013.

and Horner (along with a bunch of children whose summer vacation had been hijacked for the cause) mapped out the Gold Coast – for architecture, using architecture's own borrowed tools. They photographed its buildings and streetscapes with a range of equipment (including, too, a Nikon F2 and a 6 × 7 Pentax),[5] gathered ephemera, newspapers, magazines and various other materials to inform their study. It was all intended for a book on the subject that would have responded, from the Antipodes, to the Las Vegas 'discovered' by Venturi, Scott Brown, Izenour and their students. Horner and

Styant-Browne would map out the area of study and direct its analysis; Gollings would lead photography; while Jame would work on the drawings and book layout. The book project was rigorously conceived in the model of *Learning from Las Vegas* but did not see the light of day. At the end of 1974, Styant-Browne faced the decision to sign on for a further five-year contract at Lae or to move on, and choosing the latter he moved, as he has put it, from Lae to LA, taking up graduate studies at the University of California at the start of a decade-long American sojourn. The book followed him across the Pacific, but failed to

7.7 & 7.8 John Gollings, Pool and Gardens,
El Dorado Motel, Surfers Paradise, 1974/
Drive-exit, Crowne Plaza Hotel, Surfers
Paradise, 2013.

eventuate as his professional career took off and the
neon of Surfers Paradise dimmed with distance.[6]

Boyd's comments on Surfers Paradise in *The
Australian Ugliness* presaged the first major attempt
to subject the Gold Coast to architectural criticism:
the articles and editorials of the *Gold Coast* issue
of *Architecture in Australia*. Offered in the mode of
a 'townscape' architectural criticism, the city is

presented as a problem in perspective and plan. By asserting greater controls in architecture and town planning, it might yet have been remedied: stronger architectural involvement in everyday building types; cultural criticism of the pop surface; identification of general lessons for the Australian city from the particular circumstances of Surfers Paradise and the Gold Coast. The *Strategic Plan* developed by Clarke,

Gazzard and Associates for the Gold Coast City Council in 1969 effectively offered a formal response from within the problem of setting out the lines for the city's future development. The *Learning from Surfers Paradise* project, as it has come to be known, was an entirely different mode of analysis. Born from the same stock as Boyd's criticism, it was a question instead of understanding the city on its own terms,

7.9 & 7.10 John Gollings, El Rancho Bar-B-Q,
Corner of Ferny Avenue and Cavill Avenue,
Surfers Paradise, 1974/Circle on Cavill Fashion
Dining, Corner of Ferny Avenue and Cavill
Avenue, Surfers Paradise, 2013.

in the moment and without judgment (though never entirely). It made a claim upon the post-war city, and then the postmodern city as problems for architecture. As such, it is the second major assessment made by architectural culture of the Gold Coast after the attention it received at the end of the 1950s and survives as a photographic survey.

To this survey, another layer has been added. Significantly, the project was taken up again, nearly forty years later, as a rephotography project by John Gollings, titled *Learning from Surfers Paradise, 1973/2013*, in which the city as it had stood in 1974 received renewed attention, and in which the twenty-first century city invited fresh discussion.[7] The project took up the immediate lessons of the Las Vegas project and ran these through the additional filters of hindsight and change: what was the city of this moment, and what did it become? In its two Australian outings (at the Gold Coast Art Gallery in 2013 and the

7.11 & 7.12 John Gollings, Pacific Ocean and Surfers Paradise, latitude S 27° 59' 51.15", longitude E 153° 26' 15.258", altitude 303m, 1974/2013.

RMIT Design Hub in Melbourne in 2014) the Gollings show was paired with the exhibition *Las Vegas Studio* (curated by Hilar Stadler and Martino Stierli), which explored the artefacts of the original 1968 study that gave rise to *Learning from Las Vegas*.[8] In the Gold Coast staging of these two projects, especially, both the Gold Coast and Las Vegas were treated as cities in conversation with one another – rather than conversations between two analytical projects.

In his rephotography, John Gollings revisited the images taken in January 1974 along with Styant-Browne, Jame and Horner, using, where possible, the same lenses and contemporary variations on the same techniques – not to mention his extensive field notes – to reshoot images of Surfers Paradise from the same positions and at the same scale. The nature of rephotography (or, recalling its origins in geology, 'repeat photography') is to document change, a gesture that can never be undertaken

7.13 & 7.14 John Gollings, TraveLodge, Surfers Paradise, 1974/The Islander Resort, looking west from the corner of Beach Road, Surfers Paradise, 2013.

without inviting judgment on that very change. In this, the Swiss and Australian shows were on a different conceptual footing. *Learning from Surfers Paradise 1973–2013* occupied the lower gallery of the Gold Coast City Gallery with a clear then-and-now message, while the upper gallery housed *Las Vegas Studio*, for which then and now was a question of the means of analysis rather than its subject.

Among elements of *Learning from Surfers Paradise* was Styant-Browne's own copy of *Learning from Las Vegas*, as well as a small modicum of correspondence and documentation from the 1974 field study and its preparations in the months prior. Gollings's images trace the dramatic scale shift to which the Gold Coast in general and Surfers Paradise in particular (not to mention the adjacent canal estates off the

Nerang River) had been subject over these four decades. The overwhelming image conveyed in the exhibition was of a city that had exceeded the scale of its analysis in the 1970s. A pair of photographs depicting a freestanding 1950s motel (the El Dorado, opened in 1955) becomes, in 2013, a lobby interior, without a change in frame or position; an open field littered with a lonely sign and oil drum fills up with boxy suburban homes. Gollings documents the effects upon a city of rapid growth driven by the market forces of tourism.

In mounting a rephotography project alongside the materials of the Las Vegas studio, however, the effect is to foster precisely this nostalgia for an easy postmodernism. Las Vegas at the end of the 1960s is inevitably highly aestheticised to eyes conditioned by the gains of Andy Warhol, Ed Ruscha and the original 'Mad Men', and a corresponding image of a smaller, poorer, pop city like Surfers fosters a sense of something having been lost. These were not exhibitions of photography or urban analysis so much as reflections on the Las Vegas and Gold Coast they captured. In returning to his 1970s efforts to learn from Surfers Paradise, Gollings's work was appropriated to show how the Gold Coast was, at a certain moment, like Las Vegas, and how just as you could learn from Las Vegas, you could learn (presumably the same things, if in an Australian register) from Surfers Paradise. *Learning from Las Vegas* had demonstrated that the trajectory of that city was not a sequence of very bad things so much as entirely mundane decisions and manoeuvres that had become exceptional through their amplification. In this way, *Las Vegas Studio* – documenting work from the 1960s – served to legitimate the Gold Coast project and, by extension, the Gold Coast as another exceptional city in which the normal was blown up beyond the lines of good taste that Boyd suggested had already been crossed in the 1950s. It framed a local discussion about how the Gold Coast *was*, and about how much had been *lost*.

The nostalgia implicit in this move fails, of course, to deal with the shifts to which Las Vegas itself has been subject in the intervening years, shifts that parallel the fates of any number of cities that rest so heavily on tourism, speculative development and the misbehaviour that accrues within both. It fails to account, too, for the paradox of privileging historical urban dross while at the same time ignoring its present-day manifestations as deservedly below the radar – no longer proper to the aestheticisation to which the industrial or service periphery was subject in the 1960s and 1970s. The Gold Coast Highway running through Surfers Paradise in the 1970s has a status that the light industry and big-box commerce of Brisbane Road or the Southport–Nerang Road would

7.15 & 7.16 John Gollings, Surfers Paradise Boulevard, view south, 1974/2013.

struggle to achieve in the present. The lesson of Las Vegas for the Gold Coast is much less in the form of a problem – how to read today's industrial parks or strip malls as part of a larger complex of urban phenomena; how to continue to test and expand the limits of what is worth discussing in architecture – than in the form of a stance: the Gold Coast deserves your attention, because it was once like Las Vegas and can be so again.

Reading *Learning from Surfers Paradise* against *Las Vegas Studio* nonetheless allows us to see a hitherto underappreciated value in the Lae reading of *Learning from Las Vegas* for the postmodern history of Australian architecture. The project

mounted by Horner, Jame, Gollings and Styant-Browne and the subject to which they turned have both been elevated in consequence. In the light placed on their efforts to respond directly to the lessons of Las Vegas, as presented by Venturi, Scott Brown and Izenour, the exhibitions briefly set up an eddy in a history of Australian postmodernism that has tended to prize both the local path out of modern architecture in the mode of a critical regionalism and apprenticeship in the dark arts of architectural theory at the world's discursive centres. The 1973–1974 Surfers Paradise study was a failed project in that it had no immediate impact on the Australian debate or on the Australian

7.17 & 7.18 John Gollings, Surfers Paradise Boulevard, looking south from The Shore to Apollo, 1974/to Focus and QT, Surfers Paradise, 2013.

translation of *Learning from Las Vegas*. We know it now, but at the time it was not important beyond the group who undertook the work. Except that it happened, and had been hitherto overlooked in writing the history of Australian postmodernism in which the Gold Coast acquires a substance that analysis of the 1950s and 1960s tended to resist on its behalf.

For the Australians at Lae, *Learning from Las Vegas* and the version of the Gold Coast they read through it offered a compelling variation on the studies that had distilled into their own education from the British and American architectural press as methodological sources for studying the contemporary city – not supplanting Kevin Lynch's *Image of the City* (1960) and Gordon Cullen's *Townscape* (1961), which were already in circulation during their undergraduate years and with which they were intimate, but being put into operation alongside them.[9] It celebrated an accentuated normality that would have already seemed distant to those at Lae while it would have grated with such scions of the Australian establishment as Boyd (who had died in 1971, aged 52). For Gollings, Jame, Horner and Styant-Browne, *Learning from Las Vegas* offered a clear model to apply to the closest city that taste had left behind – not Las Vegas, to be sure, but close enough.

7.19 & 7.20 John Gollings, Car Park
Surfers Paradise Hotel with Kinkabool
and Paradise Towers, view south from
Cavill Avenue, Surfers Paradise, 1974/
Body Store, Surfers Centro Arcade,
Surfers Paradise, 2013.

8.1 Atlantis (architects Heather Thiedeke Group). Paradise Waters, completed 1982.

8.2 St Vincent's Parish Centre (architects Heather Thiedeke Group), Surfers Paradise, completed 1986.

8   A Profession Organised

The decision to establish the Gold Coast Architecture Awards in 1984 responded to a timely confluence of motivations and circumstances affecting the Gold Coast city-region and its architects. It also offers a lens on the consolidation of the architecture profession across the 1970s and 1980s. The previous decade had seen tremendous growth in the permanent and temporary populations of the southeast corner of Queensland and its coastal cities in particular, provoking a substantial high-rise building boom centred on Main Beach and Surfers Paradise. The number of architects actively working on the Gold Coast more than doubled in this time. The professional landscape transformed from one in which architects were in sustained competition with designer-builders to realise single family dwellings and low-rise tourism accommodation to one dominated by the design and construction of high-rise towers, which even when realised in the manner of a casual approach to property development necessitated the architect's technical expertise. The Gold Coast's architects nonetheless needed to position themselves publicly in a moment when the effects of their practice were becoming decidedly more public: not simply for designing bespoke houses and monumental moments in a city that had clearly taken off – and would, it rightly seemed, continue to do so – but also for the sheer volume of projects that was

shaping the morphology of the city and marking out the lines of its future development.

In designing apartment towers, resorts, shopping malls, casinos and theme parks, architects were re-drafting the city's skyline, which consequently changed year to year. And while setting out to prove something to the city's population and those who saw scope for investment opportunities along its golden beaches, the Gold Coast Division of what was then the Royal Australian Institute of Architects (RAIA) also took on the task of reversing the image maintained elsewhere in Australia of the Gold Coast as a cultural dead spot. The Gold Coast Architecture Awards were self-styled from Southport to Coolangatta as the Architectural Oscars and they conducted battle on two fronts: to demonstrate the value of the work of architects on the Gold Coast to this adolescent city; and to prove the worth of the Gold Coast to a national architectural culture that had weighed it in the balance and found it curious, but wanting. Gold Coast architects were making a city and in a culture of experimentation free of any kind of resistance in which anything was possible.

In this objective, the Gold Coast had to contend with a reputation that had formed around it over the course of the 1950s and 1960s. The first iteration of the awards came twenty-five years after the RAIA had made its most comprehensive formal assessment of the city. As already recalled in the first chapter of this book, on the eve of their inauguration, Neville

**8.3 Golden Grove Retirement Village
(architects Heather Thiedeke Group),
Southport, completed 1983.**

Gruzman, who was long an advocate for improved public space and amenity in his own city, suggested that the Gold Coast would best be served by a convoy of concerned architects in bulldozers, heading north from the civilised centres and pushing Surfers Paradise into the sea. It was a city best treated as an experiment gone awry. The Gold Coast press and the Division's members gave this suggestion the attention it demanded, translating a call for a fresh start into a touchstone for a determined effort to lift the local game so as to prove Gruzman and his co-belligerents wrong. Indeed, invited to comment on the occasion of the tenth and twentieth Gold Coast Architecture Awards, Gruzman conceded that much had already been done to attend to those of the city's failings that had prompted his suggestion of 1984, even if there remained some distance to go in improving the city's urban design as the city itself continued to grow at an ever-accelerated rate. Gruzman's assessment represented a wider view, but it was seen as overly patronising; a quick, down-the-nose and across-the-border judgment. Speaking in 2013, local architect Malcolm Cummings, whose practice was largely focused on Gold Coast projects, offered a mirror to the city's critics: 'It's interesting how architects would come up to the Gold Coast and criticise the buildings. There are a lot of buildings in Sydney you could say could be bulldozed into the sea.'[1]

The Gold Coast Division of the RAIA had been established as a way to bring together the small number of architects working on the Gold Coast in (to quote architect Bill Heather), 'a structured way'. It also offered a chance to push back against the negative perceptions of the city and its architecture that had been fostered throughout Australia. In a speech to the twentieth anniversary dinner of the Gold Coast Architecture Awards in 2003 (reprinted in the locally published *20/20 Vision*), Heather recalled that when he arrived to set up an office of Melbourne firm of Buchan, Laird and Bawden in 1972, there were a mere dozen architects on the Coast, 'thinly spread between Coolangatta to Southport.' He recites a list: Col Merrin and Owen Ryan in Coolangatta, Robert Cummings (Emeritus Professor of Architecture at the University of Queensland) and his aforementioned son Malcolm Cummings (with an office at Surfers Paradise), Russ Gibbons at Mermaid Beach, Noel Edser and Bevan Whittington (Design Collaborative) on Chevron Island, George Dunlop and David Raby (working together with Heather at Buchan, Laird and Bawden in Surfers Paradise), Andris Stenders, Ron Burling and John Mobbs (all at the Southport office of Clarke, Gazzard and Associates), as well as Les Nyerges, an architect with the Gold Coast City Council.[2]

As a member of the RAIA's National Membership Committee, Heather was in regular contact with the Queensland Chapter President David Phillips, who

8.4 Millroys Jewellers (architects Heather Thiedeke Group), Scarborough Fair Shopping Centre, Southport, completed 1984.

encouraged the small group then comprising the Gold Coast Area Committee to consider the example that had been set by the geographically vast North Queensland Division and to establish a Gold Coast Division – even using the North Queensland articles of association as the basis for the Gold Coast's documents, which were adapted, as Heather recalled 'to suit our needs'. While its geographical reach would expand with time, the Pimpama River was established as the initial northern border, with the state line defining the Division's southern boundary and the western border taking in Mount Tamborine and the city's hinterland.

Looking back on the atmosphere of this moment, John Mobbs had this to say in 2013: 'It wasn't as serious and heavy as it was in the cities, and I think there was a bit of jealousy because they weren't having the same fun that we were having up here. Clients were more ready to accept more innovative solutions to projects. Also, a lot happened here in a very short time.' The comparison was more often than not with the southern cities of Sydney and Melbourne rather than with Brisbane, which struggled with its own reputation as a provincial hub as much as the Gold Coast wrestled with its reputation as the nation's capital of tackiness. Given the pace of development in the border city, however, competition for work was fierce and the local profession worked hard to secure its place. The Huntingdon Club offered a venue for the small Gold Coast Area Committee and its constituency to meet on a regular basis, a practice carried forward as the Gold Coast Division was established. According to the younger Cummings: 'The Huntington Club provided a marvellously talented international chef, though we couldn't figure how he came to be stuck at the Huntington. And a wonderful cellar. It really was a marvellous cellar! We had some very good nights. There are some great stories, though none of them are about architecture. There was never much discussion about architecture.'[3]

The Division's numbers had ballooned from the middle of the 1970s as a sustained development boom and a significant population rise saw 160 new towers of ten floors or more storeys built across a twelve-year period (as a slightly unbalanced point of comparison, the number of buildings of twelve storeys and above would reach 216 by 2004). Economic conditions were favourable for the scale and pace of this development, especially in light of a decision by the Queensland Government in 1977 to waive death duties that saw an extraordinarily high and rather sudden investment in rental and vacation property from the southern states.

'[Each] new project', recalled Heather, 'seemed to result in more local offices being set up by metropolitan or interstate firms, and once they were here, and their projects completed, these architects inevitably went into practice for themselves.' Projects were overwhelmingly in the genre of high-rise residential development, with increased attention, into the 1980s, to precinct planning and the development of city infrastructure. Such firms as Burling Brown and the Davis Heather Group (later Heather Thiedeke) were 'producing interesting high rise apartments', and Conrad & Gargett and Bill Job & Associates maintained 'strong local offices'. Recalled Heather: 'The profession was in good shape, and architectural design was making a difference to the look of the city.'

A 'portfolio of experiments', as Philip Follent has put it, the Gold Coast at once offered a challenge to good taste and a model for the architect's unbridled optimism. If this was true of Gold Coast architecture more broadly – and especially in the form and immediate urbanism of the residential tower – then it was particularly so in the work the profession itself put forward for the Gold Coast Architecture Awards. The programme was born out of a wish to demonstrate the best work of the Gold Coast's architecture profession. It would, though, come to define the character of the Division (ten years old at their outset) and defend a form of originality and variety it held to be its own – a rare instance from the 1980s of architects and developers sharing the page. It defined, too, the relationship between the Gold Coast and Queensland more broadly, as well as with Australia and the cities, regions and countries against which it could legitimately define itself, which across its history would span from Miami to Honolulu to Dubai.

8.5 Sports Marine (architects Media Five),
Main Beach, completed 1988.

8.6 Currumbin Engineering Administration
Centre and Factory Building (architects
Cummings and Burns), Currumbin, 1983–84.

8.7 St Kevin's Catholic Primary School
(architects Davis Heather Group),
Benowa, 1977–79.

In a talk to the 1978 RAIA's Queensland Chapter Convention 'Insite/Outsight', Bill Heather emphasised the distinctiveness of Gold Coast architecture within the state's professional and cultural landscape. Speaking, he said, as 'a provincial observer from that area you regard as a kind of "architectural purgatory",' he thought Brisbane architecture could use 'a dose of the sunshine and sensuality associated with the Coast.' Reflecting on the relationship of the new Gold Coast Division to the Queensland Chapter ('we are small cheese to you city slickers'), he observed:

> There is good reason why Brisbane is the branch office capital of Australia and why its architects suffer from a kind of "architectural colonialism": even if some of the empires are staffed by natives recruited in the colony, sluggish as they may be. The two main problems confronting the Institute here today are inertia and complacency. Inertia because there is a great resistance to change and

lack of momentum in the way things are done. Complacency because there is a lack of outward vision about what could be done. We are in the right place at the right time, but our sights are set too low and no one cares. We are at the threshold of the most challenging period of this State's growth.[4]

Heather asserted that Queensland as a whole and Brisbane in particular had let pass the opportunity to realise a moment akin to that faced by Chicago in the 1880s, but that the (Queensland) Gold Coast was not, for better or worse, prepared to do so. 'Impatience and ambition should be the order of the day – a restructuring of our activities should attempt to tap the vitality of the small cell rather than let the inertia of the large organism choke the system.' Inviting his audience to 'substitute personal action for collective inertia', he offered the Gold Coast as an example to the state. If Queensland architecture were only prepared to loosen ties, shed vests and trade lethargy for an optimism prepared to absorb mistakes as it moved insistently forward, 'we on the Gold Coast will offer you encouragement periodically and example where necessary.'[5]

The city was hardly invisible to the rest of the State and, indeed, Gold Coast projects had from time to time done well in the Queensland Architecture Awards (if not nationally). Hayes and Scott's Pfitzenmaier Beach House had been given an award for its merits by the Queensland Institute of Architects in the mid-1950s, and their Miller House in Southport – with its gold-coloured front door – had been named Queensland House of the Year in 1965. The early 1970s had seen The Anchorage (fig. 8.8, designed by Clarke, Gazzard and Associates in conjunction with the Hawaiian firm of Belt, Collins and Associates at Budds Beach) receive an award at state level. But the relationship between local recognition and performance in the state or national architecture awards was not direct, with each competition searching for different qualities in the works it held up as exemplary. Not all projects were submitted for consideration, and the Seidler-designed apartments (1978–82) in Broadbeach Waters, for instance, almost escapes recognition in

the local architectural landscape. Simply speaking, the Gold Coast Architecture Awards were judged on criteria that shifted from year to year, responding to the evolving opportunities and problems faced by Gold Coast architects as they went about their work. And until their regularisation within a state-wide regional awards cycle, the Gold Coast Architecture Awards rewarded that work, in particular, that took the city with it.

The role of publicist Ken Newton and journalist Brian Mossop in promoting the awards cannot be overstated. Nor can their part in the achievement of the programme's ambitions. With Newton's guidance, especially, the Gold Coast Division affected a meaningful engagement with the public, and the *Gold Coast Bulletin* (where Mossop was on staff) maintained its long-standing interest in issues around architecture, development and the city – for many years being represented on the State-appointed jury by its editor or other senior staff, and often Mossop himself. Newton and Mossop saw the need to shape the way the public

8.8 The Anchorage (architects Clarke Gazzard, with Belt Collins and Associates), Budds Beach, 1972.

8.9 Jansen Residence (architects Peter Jansen and Associates), Carrara, completed 1986.

understood and valued both the architecture profession and those issues directly shaping the city and its fabric. They sought to shift the public perception of the architect's contribution to the Gold Coast for the better. The Division produced a guide to engaging an architect's services as a direct marketing effort, but its public presence was most directly felt in the clear and impassioned communiqués issued by Newton's media office on behalf of the Gold Coast Division of the Institute. The Awards took what the architects were doing and built up its popular image among the Gold Coast public while affording the local profession a chance to take a very public stance on the kind of architectural work that deserved the recognition and praise that the public, thanks to Newton and Mossop, were now prepared to give it. This clearly raised the stakes for the Gold Coast architecture fraternity, since with opportunities for innovation and experimentation came, too, the possibility of a highly visible endorsement or a silent reprimand from an architect's peers.

The benchmarks were in each year set by a jury comprising architects from within and beyond the region and members of both the building industry and an engaged public. For the first decade, spanning from the inception of the awards to their incorporation into a State awards programme

feeding the Queensland Architecture Awards, decisions were taken by a jury of three, ordinarily comprising two members of the Gold Coast Division and a third juror drawn from outside the region. In these first years the Gold Coast Division appointed each jury and the decisions it took did not affect a project's capacity to be entered into the state-level competition (which fed, naturally enough, into the national architecture awards).[6]

The jury was responsible for visiting each submission and holding a discussion in which projects were held up for examination against criteria that were, in part, treated as natural, but which year by year revealed the preoccupations of the jury. What makes a work of architecture good? Why does one project deserve an award over the others? Or the judges' commendation? The answers were many and varied: detailing, response to context, response to brief, budgetary responsibility, economic impact, attention to environmental impact, expression of the landscape, expression of lifestyle, expression of the city, and on it went. Is good Gold Coast architecture especially good if it would also be considered good elsewhere (where elsewhere, more often than not, meant Brisbane)? Taken year by year the relationship between the values given away in the jury summations and premiated projects is not difficult to map, but the overall picture is of a series of juries understanding the role of the awards as being to move the city forward by rewarding the rendering public the best examples of architectural practice. The awards did not track fashion (although they arguably did this, too) so much as they plotted new ideas – ostensibly focusing on the future rather than the present, and on the capacity of the profession in its entirety as revealed in the work submitted for review.

The inaugural Gold Coast Architecture Awards received thirty-four submissions from practices on the Gold Coast and beyond. The work submitted spanned across all building types, from private houses to restaurant interiors to public buildings, and offered what the Institute itself called 'a cross-section of the Gold Coast lifestyle.' Projects had to

PERSPECTIVE

8.10 Greenmount Guest House (architects Burling Brown and Partners), Coolangatta, completed 1981.

have been realised (and substantially completed) in the five-year period leading up to a submission deadline of April 1984. As announced by the RAIA, submissions could 'cover any architectural works including restored and recycled buildings, interior design, exhibition design, public utilities, and recreational design.' Recognition was, in these inaugural awards, made on the basis of several category distinctions. The reconstructed Greenmount Beach Resort, by architects Burling Brown and Partners (fig. 8.10), received the award in the high-rise category, while in the low-rise, awards went to the Abri Home for the Aged in Southport, by Brisbane architects Conrad & Gargett (fig. 8.11), and to St Kevin's Catholic Primary School at Benowa, by the Davis Heather Group – with St Kevin's (see fig. 8.7), a fine example of postmodern humanism, going on to receive a Queensland Architecture Award for civic design. Malcolm Cummings secured the best house award for the Geraghty Residence at Nerang, while in the interior

category, recently-established Gold Coast office of Honolulu-headquartered Media Five (under Desmond Brooks) was recognised for its work on Cavill's Restaurant, part of the reconstructed Tiki Village development at Surfers Paradise. Several 'runners up' were named in each class, including Follent's house in the McPherson Ranges (fig. 8.12), which went on to win the Queensland House of the Year. An exhibition of drawings, photographs and models was put up at the City Council premises in Evandale, including a model of the Conrad International Hotel and Jupiter's Casino (as it was initially named, by Buchan, Laird and Bawden, fig. 8.13) – its design architect, Nicholas Water, was a juror, and it was not given an award. An exhibition of twenty models was then shown at the Community Arts Centre in Edward Street, Brisbane. This exhibition was supplemented by a lecture programme by Gold Coast architects at the University of Queensland and scaffolded by the constant presence during exhibition opening hours of Gold Coast Division members, who remained 'on hand to explain their approach to Gold Coast Architecture.'[7]

If Gruzman had a year earlier given Gold Coast architects a point to prove, in 1985 juror Ian Douglas of the Victorian firm of Suendermann Douglas McFall evidently set out to keep the region's architects on their toes. A former partner of Roy Grounds and well versed in large-scale civic projects, he observed to the *Gold Coast Bulletin* that the architecture of Surfers Paradise, in particular, was a 'fun and resort type architecture. This is a fun place and it produces fun architecture, not necessarily good architecture. There is little greatness or exhilaration about the architecture, although it is difficult to produce brilliant

8.11 Abri Home for the Aged (architects Conrad & Gargett), Southport, 1980–83.

8.12 Greatorix Residence (architect Philip Follent), McPherson Ranges, completed 1983.

buildings in this resort climate. However,' he conceded, 'what is bad architecture to some is good to others.'

It is worth noting, here, that the region's architects were not simply processing an unending boom. Although the early 1980s had been kind to the profession, a sudden downturn in new investment and construction in the middle of the decade stripped firms of work. Michael Jones recalls an article from *Time* magazine in 1982 heralding the 'cooling down' of the Gold Coast as a tourist destination, reflecting the lag between tourist numbers and the provision of infrastructure. As the *Bulletin* itself noted in May 13 of that year, such resort towns as 'Acapulco, Waikiki, Miami Beach and Nice' were 'built around the natural, environment resources of sun and surf. People were originally attracted to these places because of the excellent combination of these essential beach resort ingredients. As the word got out and more people were attracted to these ideal holiday areas, the entrepreneurs responded with often minimal accommodation and facilities.'[8]

The following year's jury likewise felt obliged to offer a diagnosis of the city alongside judgments of its architecture. In a press release entitled 'Jurors in Judgment', the RAIA made this comment on the eve of the 1986 Gold Coast Architecture Awards: 'Gold Coast buildings are either loved or loathed, and over the years, the city has suffered more than its share of critics. Local architects, however, are going all out to prove that the tourist resort does have heart and soul – and plenty of beautiful buildings to match its beautiful people.' The previous year's awards, and Douglas's assessment in particular, had presented an early setback in the quest to secure for Gold Coast architects due recognition of their work. But the Institute described this third iteration of the local awards as 'another salvo in their campaign to be recognised as a major force in the moulding of the Gold Coast of the future.' Consolidating the increased profile the awards had secured for the region's architects, Division Chair Peter Clarke launched a brochure at the awards reception to further this task. Called *Architects Designing the Future*, it argued for the

8.13 Aerial view of Jupiter's Casino and Broadbeach Island, Broadbeach, c.1987 (architects Buchan, Laird and Bawden, completed 1986).

central role played by the architect in improving the city's quality – and reinforced the function of the awards as a tool for asserting the profession's importance for urban-scale considerations. Of the overall quality of the projects to receive citations in the 1986 Gold Coast Architecture Awards, the jury had this to say: 'A robust regional style seems to be emerging, expressed in architecture in as many different ways as there are lifestyles – some florid, some restrained, always alert and often adventurous. The new generation of development is of sufficient quality now that it should silence those former critics and cultural cringers who used to enjoy knocking the Gold Coast. This region can now strike back with evidence of architecture.'[9]

This professional resilience in the face of criticism would continue to inform the position taken by the group actively practising in the city.

By 1987, with three rounds of awards already made, the divisional cycle had already done much to enhance public appreciation of architectural quality in the region and to undo the image – maintained throughout the state and beyond – of the Gold Coast as a designer's backwater. As local members of the RAIA conceded: 'In one of Australia's fastest growing cities which less than three decades ago was little more than a collection of holiday homes and cow pastures, it has been hard to find an architectural individuality, so rapid has been the change.' Architect Don Williamson observed that 'there was still a long way to go ... [We] hope architects will enrich the nature of the city by continuing their search for that ideal ... [The] Gold Coast must be future oriented rather than reflective of its past.' (In this vein, Williamson took the opportunity to express his avid support for a proposed monorail project that would 'have the greatest impact on the city since the late Sir Bruce Small dug his first canal.') As the jurors noted in their official statement, they were 'interested in architecture that had an expressive imagery and conveyed a central idea or plot beyond solving the functional or technical problems. 'In other words', they continued, 'we would hope that architects will further enrich the nature of the city here, and would continue their search. This could include further experimentation and the integration of high technology.'[10]

To 1988: 'Architects on the Gold Coast have drawn the line', declared jury chairman Alan Hayes. 'The city is no longer just a branch office for big companies and professional groups. Instead of being out on a limb in the design industry Coast architects are exporting their expertise around Australia and overseas.' Hayes estimated the net value of projects being designed by Gold Coast architects in the Solomon Islands, Perth, Adelaide and Darwin to be in the neighbourhood of A$2.6 million. 'I feel that the architects led the way in turning the branch office image around on the Gold Coast and now we are seeing national and even multi-nationals set up head offices here ... It's the Californian sunbelt syndrome all over. The city is becoming more and more sophisticated on a broader base than just tourism and property development but it is in these areas that the greatest impact has occurred in the changing

8.14 Sheraton Mirage (architects Media Five), Main Beach, completed 1987.

image. [It] was only a few years ago that Coast architects were seen as having to survive on their local products.' Brisbane-based juror Geoffrey Pie warned local architects not to 'kill the goose that laid the golden egg', speaking at the awards dinner in front of Gold Coast Mayor Alderman Lex Bell and Albert Shire President Bill Laver. 'There is', he continued, 'an immense tussle between foreign design influences, especially American, and the traditional Queensland spirit in the city.' His comments surely invoked the pool of award-winning projects. The sole architecture award made in 1988 was to Media Five's project for the Sheraton Mirage (fig. 8.14), continuing a run of recognition by the Gold Coast office of the multinational firm and its principal, Desmond Brookes and recognising the importance of the Raptis development project – the twin of which, across the road, would also receive recognition in the following year.[11]

Ahead of the weekend in which entries for the 1989 Gold Coast Architecture Awards went on public display at Evandale, jury chair Ron Burling signalled his intention to use the occasion of the awards to offer some broad reflections on the state and prospects of the Gold Coast. 'Many Gold Coast buildings that were developed to satisfy the needs of the 1970s and 1980s', he suggested in an RAIA media release, 'will be demolished to make way for the needs of the 1990s … [It] will be necessary to redevelop much of the "not-so-old" development on the Gold Coast. It will have to be done to cater for future permanent and tourist population.' Both the city's fixed and its transient population would, he asserted, continue to rise – just as the Gold Coast's population had increased more than ten-fold from the time of his arrival in 1957 to 1989 (and by a further three-fold since) – and neither the architectural stock of the city nor its infrastructure was yet ready for what would come. 'These problems need to be seriously addressed and planned for today.'

In Burling's reflections on the Gold Coast as a whole, he recalled how he had watched – and indeed helped – the Gold Coast's rapid growth as it tracked, and in part overcame, the problems experienced by 'the waterways of Florida, the hotel

8.15 Gold Coast International Hotel, (architects Media Five), Surfers Paradise, completed 1985.

lay-outs of Las Vegas and the high-rises of Miami and Hawaii.' Architects had learned the lesson that building rapidly does not allow projects to receive 'the necessary amount of artistic consideration' and that these quickly fail the test of 'perennial debate.' Observed Burling in reflecting on the awards: 'Since the Gold Coast awoke from its sleepy seaside town existence, its whole future has evolved around being different, attracting attention and setting new trends … Of course, there are those examples of jarring taste that give rise to the claim of "brash and brassy". But the conservative view tends to exaggerate the number of these buildings.'[12]

In a statement released by the Gold Coast division of the RAIA, 1991 Gold Coast Architecture Awards jury chair, Evan Winkle of Media Five, credited a 'new sophistication' in Gold Coast architecture 'with increasing the number of foreign tourists visiting the coastal strip.' He suggested that 'the quality of architecture over recent years has put the Gold Coast on equal footing with its major resort competitors – Hawaii and South-East Asia. The increase in foreign investment has allowed a gradual emergence of sophistication in Gold Coast architecture ... The continual search for excellence in architecture, promoted by these annual awards, has allowed the Gold Coast to be seen as a serious competitor with other popular destinations. He went on to observe: 'Over recent years, Gold Coast architecture has progressed from home unit developments to the international hotel market, on to integrated resorts and the planning of new regional communities. By rewarding design excellence, the awards have helped foster a strong sense of professionalism and innovation among Gold Coast architects. They have also led to an increased demand for quality, architecturally-designed residential homes. People see the visual appeal of the architecturally-designed international hotels and integrated resorts and want the same quality and finish, as well as the individual style, for their own home.'[13]

Within a decade of their establishment the Gold Coast awards would set the standard for the RAIA's Queensland Chapter. In 1992 Queensland adopted the Gold Coast Division's model for the state awards program and rolled it out across all the Queensland regions. This was hailed as a great coup for Gold Coast, which had demonstrated the value of rewarding work at a regional level, but it became quickly apparent that there was little room left for regional distinctions. The enthusiastic group that had seen the Gold Coast Architecture Awards established and worked to secure their local importance was obliged to give way to policies, procedures and judgment criteria intended to make the awards process manageable and consistent across the entire state, leaving little room for variety, originality, spontaneity or the kind of specificity demanded by the Gold Coast as a setting for architectural design.

Nonetheless, the awards continued to provide a regular opportunity for reflection on the specific problems of architectural practice in the Gold Coast, given the conditional independence of its economic cycles and the dominance of the relationship between architects and developers. In his summary of deliberations in 1994 – a cycle that includes the curious Tange Residence at Paradise Waters (fig. 8.16, Patane Group, for the Japanese architect Kenzo Tange and his family) – Gold Coast architect Eldon Bottcher could thus seize the occasion to describe the Gold Coast as 'raw, lusty, vigorous, energetic and raunchy' – qualities to be embraced rather than overcome. 'A city which has developed so rapidly cannot possibly mature too early. It will go through a number of transition stages. While it might lack grace and subtlety, its "difference" is something to celebrate. It's going to be an interesting exercise to follow the progress of the region as it matures through the years. The Gold Coast is developing a very distinctive flavour which, at the end of the day, will be vital to its future as an international tourist destination – we can't all be refined cities and neither should we attempt to emulate them. If you lost the lusty environment you would lose what Surfers Paradise is all about. It's the right thing but done in a very raw way. It is part of our transition to maturity.'[14]

Five years later, the field suggested new kinds of problems, responding to a different set of conditions shaping a practice that had embraced with renewed vigour the full range of formal and decorative possibilities suggested by the postmodern turn. In his capacity as the regional awards chair, Denis Holland argued: '[we] must remind ourselves that in this industry the greatest risk is letting the 'mediocre' stand as the visible representation of our most recent work. All the buildings on display tonight have qualities which set them apart. They are *good* buildings. I'm using the plain-English word "good" intentionally, because we as architects don't find easy agreement when using words such as stylish, evocative, inspiring, even functional.' He suggested that the work lies in finding the balance between 'the engagingly evocative' and 'the trowelled-on pastiche', 'the stage sets' and 'the substance', and a building that is strong, but the 'architecture' of which 'gets blown off in each cyclone.' But, as he

8.16 Tange Residence (Patane Group),
Paradise Waters, completed 1993.

continued, 'the real danger occurs when "looking backward" becomes the major focus ... Surgeons don't do a "baroque style caesarean section" and we don't have "Mediterranean" jumbo jets with Tuscan doors.'[15]

These thoughts occupy the realm of hyperbole, but the anxiety behind them echoes those voices of earlier decades that looked with disdain or horror at those works realised under the banner of architecture. In this sense, it is telling that in this same year the Building of the Year Award was made to the Daryl Jackson Architects-designed Couran Cove development (fig. 8.17), 'a maritime village resort located within the Broadwater with direct access to the sand dune landscape of South Stradbroke Island.' The jury regarded the challenges of scale and composition as being 'masterfully handled resulting in ... a resort with an exceptional emphasis on environmental responsibility.' The jury cast this project as a moment of respite from the Coast's unrelenting growth: 'This is the Gold Coast's alter ego or its conscience. The Gold Coast is an enjoyable place, but its activity is going to be happily contained by a protective rung of environmentally sound development such as Couran Cove with its intricate environmental sustainability and energy efficiency.'[16] (Subjected over time to the logic of tourism, the Couran Cove resort would ultimately be forced to close its doors, its prestige units turned over to the low-cost rental market.[17])

8.17 Couran Cove Resort (Daryl Jackson Architects), South Stradbroke Island, completed 1998.

In the mid-1990s the Gold Coast Division was re-structured into a Region – more directly accountable to the Queensland Chapter – that also quickly accommodated the Northern Rivers region in New South Wales within what had been increasingly recognised as a coherent cross-border architectural culture. The Gold Coast itself was undergoing change at the same time, substantially increasing its municipal geography and population in the amalgamation of the Gold Coast with Albert River Shire in 1994 – necessitating a fresh approach to city planning and management that had direct implications for the role of architects both in private practice and in relation to the significantly enlarged, and conspicuously less laissez-faire, Gold Coast City Council. All of this affected the momentum of architectural production and public debate and introduced new accountabilities in both procedure and the values shaping architectural quality. The energy, speed and the qualities Heather had espoused in 1978 could no longer set the tone in what had become an inexorable tendency towards greater regulation, both in local architects' relationship with their Institute and in the city as an environment for architectural experimentation.

The city grew enormously in these middle years and so did the numbers of architects practising on the Gold Coast. Those still actively engaged and advocating for Gold Coast architects and architecture, though, found themselves regularly feeling hamstrung in their ability to shape the direction of the Gold Coast and Northern Rivers Region – to retain the character of the group that had established the Institute's presence on the Gold Coast in the early years. As the number and profile of architects and practices was growing and changing, so too was the city. The regional focus shifted away from the direct public engagement fostered by Newton and Mossop to engagement with the Gold Coast City Council and Tweed Shire Council – with their various stakeholders and an increasingly dominant planning profession. The regional group, of their own accord, took an active role in encouraging the City of Gold Coast Council to establish an urban design advisory board for the city, which when established opened the way for the appointment of a City Architect and the

8.18 Albert Shire Administration Building (architects Stenders and Partners), Nerang, 1986–87.

establishment of a Council-driven awards cycle to reward the best instances of urban design, which had the dual effects of attending to public space and lending urban managers the tools to extend their controls into the public sphere by means previously unavailable to them.[18]

As the guest of honour at the Gold Coast (and Northern Rivers) thirtieth annual regional awards (2013), Michael Bryce – an architect and Gold Coast native – chastised the 'literati' and their scorn of 'the decorative nature of the Gold Coast's early "motel" architecture … eminently suited [as it was] to the strong sunlight and pastel surfaces – a playfulness that in its kitsch somehow was truthful to its role as a resort town.' Yet the Gold Coast had become aware of its own heritage, and even influenced, he noted, by the character it sought to distil from it. The challenge, we well surmise, is to take Gold Coast architecture seriously on its own terms, which was led by the city's architects themselves asserting and articulating the importance of their work therein. The 1990s had closed out a period of construction free of significant design oversight, but it ushered in a new era influenced by layered planning. In this, the history of the architectural profession and the history of urban design tell rather different, ultimately competing stories about the city.

9.1 Two men standing at the Helensvale
Railway Station sign, July 1964.

9.2 Believed to be the first home of the
Howes family, west of the Helensvale
plantation, *c*.1870.

9 Community Planning

In that same speech to the Gold Coast and Northern Rivers Regional Architecture Awards, Michael Bryce offered a tale of two cities. The Gold Coast architectural community was on that occasion marking the thirtieth cycle of the region's own architectural awards event (as we have just seen); and this in the same year as the nation's capital, Canberra, was marking the centenary of its famous inception. 'While Surfers began as a fun place', Bryce observed, 'it now wants to be taken seriously. And while Canberra began as a conservative home for bureaucrats, it now wants to be fun.'[1] The comparison holds water, especially in light of the Gold Coast's efforts to establish its cultural bona fides through the project to expand the city's arts centre into a landmark cultural precinct; and in light, too, of the swathe of building works and infrastructural improvements even then starting to spread across the city with an eye on the impending Commonwealth Games. In many respects, though, Canberra is the Gold Coast's natural counterpoint. As Michael Jones put it nearly three decades earlier: 'The Gold Coast probably tells us far more about what most Australians want than Canberra, the symbol of what bureaucrats and politicians desire.' It is, he goes on to observe, 'about Australian hopes and dreams and expectations.'[2]

While both cities vied for the Australian imagination in the middle decades of the twentieth century, one trades the plan for regulatory freedoms; regularity and institutions for a thorough going informality. The comments by both Jones in 1986 and Bryce in 2013 spoke to a tension of which the Gold Coast itself seemed aware. From the 1950s onwards developers had sought to introduce private controls over territories that had earlier attracted municipal or state-level regulation. Karl Langer's purposeful siting of dwellings in Alfred Grant's developments at Rio Vista and Miami Keys describes the architect's agency in matters beyond architecture's most obvious professional remit. (Consider, in this regard, that Langer was a close colleague in his native Vienna of Victor Grünbaum, later Victor Gruen – a pioneer in the implication of architecture in mass consumption.) Consider, too, his carefully modernistic precinct planning in Bruce Small's Paradise City, taking soft lessons from Canberra and its younger, distant cousin, Brasília, in the arrangement of various public functions. In both these cases the clarity of the initial vision was clouded by pragmatic concerns, but it did not stop successive real estate developers from proposing and founding new estates on the basis of controlled environmental values, the mutual interest of owners, and governmental self-sufficiency.

Schemes like Varsity Lakes and Sanctuary Cove have acquired a high profile in the history of planned communities on the Gold Coast, just as the vertical communities of such projects like Atlantis, at the northern end of Surfers Paradise, have fully explored the implications of the strata title legislation passed in the 1960s. To these examples can be added that of Helensvale, tracking as it does the effects of a complex large-scale vision.

In the northern part of the present-day city (until 1995 part of Albert Shire), the area now occupied by the semi-rural suburb of Oxenford and the winding streets of Helensvale had witnessed the series of trades to which the hinterland had been subject since late in the nineteenth century. By and large cleared early on of its timber stands and its Aboriginal history overwritten, the area was put to agriculture: first sugar farming, then dairy farming. A photograph of the house of the Howes family, built west of the Helensvale plantation near the present-day site of Movie World invokes a rustic, even difficult life as late as the 1870s (see fig. 9.2). Indeed, the family did poorly at farming, but found its calling as traders. The land on which their house was built was given over to an early school. A siding on the nineteenth-century Southport Express railway line eventually lent its name to the entire area (named, in turn, for early settler Helen Hessian), but until the 1970s various entrepreneurs and visionaries imagined under a series of monikers the numerous ways in which the land could be put to better use. The most noteworthy of these dates to the 1940s as an exercise in community planning in the manner of the Industrial Revolution-era mill towns of the English north – a modern response to the nineteenth-century town of Townsvale, and a poorly recognised moment in the history of planned settlements in Queensland. The property had been bought by the Davis Gelatine company, which had a factory in the vicinity, as well as farms, and in a proposal to what was, at the time, the Coomera Shire Council it sought to develop a stand-alone community settlement for its workers. These plans were not realised, however, and the land was instead sold to a cane grower named C. T. Bennett in March 1950.[3]

In April 1973, the *Gold Coast Bulletin* reported on a 'new town' project that had been approved by the Albert Shire Council (which had in 1949 absorbed Coomera Shire): an estate of 1,175 hectares for 5,000 people – bordered to the north by the Coomera River and to the south and east by the Coombabah Lake and what would, in time be reserved as the Coombabah Conservation Area. It would be called Oxenford Estates and be developed by Mainline Corporation and Alliance Holdings. The article outlined the amenities of the Estates: both rural and (sub)urban plots, 'two large neighbourhood shopping centres with full facilities'; such services as a 'post office, motel, restaurant, service station, stores, churches and schools'; 'two golf courses, equestrian area, nature areas and three man-made lakes.' A large track (400 hectares) would be set aside as open space. Urban plots were situated on elevated land to ensure that each house would enjoy a view of the lake. Mainline had realised a number of new towns and major subdivisions in the preceding years, including the mining town at Gove (Northern Territory); Pauatahanui, near Wellington (New Zealand); the urban subdivision near Macquarie University in Sydney; and condominium projects at Squaw Valley in north-east California (venue of the 1960 Winter Olympics) and Maui, in Hawaii. Despite the clarity of Mainline's plans for this area, their plans, too, would not be realised as intended.

In a report on progress dating three years later, some of the details had changed. In fact, it would be more accurate to describe the project as a fresh start, with little obvious relationship to the earlier Mainline scheme beyond its capitalisation of the landscape and its use of a central golf course as an organising device. Now called Helensvale, the community plan embraced the 'satellite town' aspects of the Oxenford Estate. (Oxenford itself was reserved for rural development, celebrated for introducing 'some fine new concepts into rural subdivisional planning.') The residential plots retained their elevation, ensuring a 'scenic outlook' over the lake for all residents. The report observed: 'Helensvale will be given a comparable treatment, except that here the developers will be working on a broader canvas and doing things on a grander scale.' In one sense a suburb arranged around two

9.3 Helensvale Golf Course Clubhouse
under construction, June 1976.

golf courses – one running through the middle of
the community, the other alongside Coombabah
Lake – it also exercised a postmodern predilection
for irregular streets and culs-de-sac as a basis for
the individualised experience of community life.
An 'uncommon street design matches the land
contours', notes the promotional material. Sold as
'a country-style open space community' in close
proximity to the established centre of Southport,
the Helensvale scheme was intended to operate as a
self-contained town for a population of around 6,500
people.[4]

The central golf course was completed in 1976 and
the first houses constructed the following year. Its
success can be measured by the difficulty with which
its dedicated realtors could keep up with demand.
Observed one at the start of 1978, consciously or
otherwise rehearsing a familiar refrain among the

city's developers: 'We have enough land to last us
through winter, but unless we bring our production
schedules forward we may not have enough for next
spring.'[5]

By October 1982, Helensvale had welcomed its
first 500 families. An article marking the milestone
in the Brisbane *Courier Mail* characterised the Estate
thus: 'Community is a key word in the Helensvale
scheme. It is neither a subdivision nor a housing
estate – the developers are building a new town,
matched on the Gold Coast only by the huge Robina
city being built further south at Merrimac.'[6] Two
years later, the Estate marked a decade since the
instigation of the first planning efforts on the
site. The Helensvale Estate Manager was on that
occasion reported in the local *Hinterlander* as
saying 'that because residential developments were
mini-societies they should be meticulously planned

9.4 Aerial view of Helensvale and
Coombabah areas, 1981.

with real concern for the long-term wellbeing of
residents.'[7] Hidden in plain view from the principal
road leading north from Surfers Paradise to
Brisbane, it was (they claimed) relatively sheltered
from sprawl by dint of its topography, while
maintaining access to the nearby urban centres of
Gold Coast and Brisbane. The Estate controlled
the community's infrastructure and amenities and
maintained strict design values.

House designs were not standardised, and
owners were free to choose any architect,
building designer, or off-the-plan scheme they
wished so long as designs were approved prior
to construction for site coverage (130 square
metres minimum), materials and permanence of
construction (no 'casual' structures, like sheds,
could be visible from the street). Speculators were
actively discouraged, leading to a high percentage
of owner-occupied dwellings.[8] All of these matters
were managed by the Helensvale Estate itself,
which was in turn a subsidiary of Sydney company
Alliance Holdings. As such, the Helensvale Estate

was a project led, from a distance, by Alliance director Sir John Overall.

A prolix profile by Doug Kennedy in the *Bulletin* presents Overall as a counterpoint to those 'soldiers and kings' who were once the world's 'empire builders'. Such figures are now supplanted by those administratively dexterous individuals who, like Overall, 'trade in the hopes and dreams of people rather than kings and tyrants, and have an instinctive knowledge of how the world should be and a shrewd idea of how to get it that way.' He had headed up the National Capital Design Commission from its foundation in 1958 to 1972, during which time much of the construction and expansion necessary to render Canberra a functioning capital city was undertaken – including the laying out of a number of the city's satellite towns, like Woden Valley and Belconnen, and the realisation of Lake Burley Griffin. Moving back into private practice in the 1970s, Overall consulted on a number of significant architectural and planning projects both in Australia and abroad, including the United Nations sponsored design of the new Tanzanian capital of Dodoma, and from 1977 on Australian Parliament House. As chair of Alliance Holdings he was at the same time overseeing the rollout of Helensvale. Noted Overall of this project: 'It has grown bigger than just another estate now. It is going to be a township with a church, primary school, shops and recreation and sporting reserves. [...] A number of people are looking for the sparkle and glamour of the Gold Coast that you find in places like Surfers Paradise, but many of the permanent population will turn to quiet country-style life at places like Nerang and here at Helensvale.'[9]

As many have noted before and since, Overall observed that the restricted paths for the city's overall expansion meant that the Gold Coast would have to densify and expand both north (past Helensvale, towards Beenleigh) and west (into the hinterland) to accommodate an inevitable growth in the region's population. Helensvale offered, in his view, a model of the balance to be found between the demands of growth and the needs of a permanent, family-focussed community. In this respect, he describes the Estate as 'the best and most professional development of its kind in Australia.'[10]

The locally published *World of Helensvale* in 1986 announced a land giveaway promotion (the '4GG Family Home') for a site on Lindfield Road – in an area then undeveloped, but since built out by a shopping centre and library linked by a road named for Overall himself. Paradise Homes collaborated with architect Malcolm Cummings on the landscape and house design, and with Helen Nugent on the interior – now all gone. During the promotion, the house would host seminars on finance, 'how to recognise your needs and wants when considering buying a new home', the process of buying a house, and various other practical considerations in investing in property.[11] It was a marker of the great Australian dream of home-ownership; and, too, of the ubiquity of this dream here as much as anywhere else.

In the years following this report the clear intentions of the Helensvale Estate were diluted by a market-driven practicality, as well by the effects on the Estate of greater connectivity to the state capital of Brisbane. By the start of 1992, the Estate marked construction of its two-thousandth home, and its final planned stage was completed in 1993 – nineteen years after the first planning consents were sought and reflecting the careful pace of development underscored by Overall himself.[12] The previous decade had seen a school opened (1984), a public house licence granted (1985) and (after some resistance) a retirement village built (announced in 1986, opened in 1988). In 1990 it had a police station. The coherence of the Estate as originally planned was undermined by rezoning that allowed for blocks of land to be secured for development by third parties, and on the back of this move Helensvale settled into its new and enduring status as a suburb of the kind that would proliferate along the northern corridor of the M1 – crossing the Coomera and Pimpama rivers in a drive north to the Albert and Logan rivers and the boundaries of Logan City – and to Helensvale's south as Arundel, Parkwood and all manner of discrete suburban developments serviced by municipal infrastructure as their population

9.5 Dreamworld from the air, 2006.

mass became critical. The thoughtful street planning of the early phases went the way of the canal estate schemes: replicating street forms and patterns without recalling their intentions beyond land efficiencies measures tested in the real estate market.

Helensvale offers an example of an estate design built around one idea of community that had already reached its zenith in the 1970s: coherent building forms and colours on an irregular street pattern, responsive to topography and popular taste, and modest (therefore) in its ambitions as

a project of architecture or urban planning. The following decade saw an iterative step further into these conservative values in the shape of the New Urbanism – by and large an American planning concept that enjoyed its most coherent expression in the Floridian towns of Seaside (from 1981) and Celebration (from 1996, a Disney town). Both aspirational and nostalgic, it invoked the language and pedestrian scale of Main Street and the values of bygone days, while attracting known designers to contribute individual works as architectural icons signalling an overall standard of design quality.

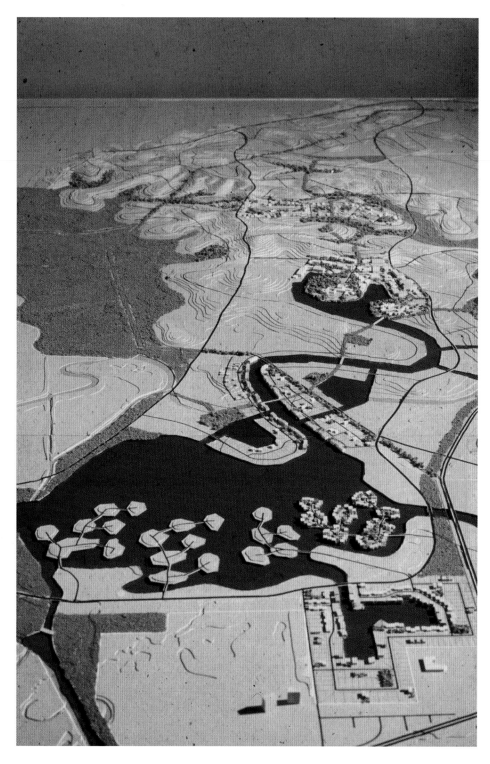

9.6 Robina New Town and Hotel-Casino
Complex, site model (Safdie Architects),
1981–82.

9.7 View towards Soho, Varsity Lakes
(design by Degenhart Shedd, 2004).

9.8 Varsity Lakes, view to Surfers
Paradise, 2014.

The community of Varsity Lakes (established 1999) was not conceived in these terms precisely. It did, though adopt them quickly and enthusiastically. Initially intended as a research park alongside Alan Bond's private university (opened 1989, masterplanned by Daryl Jackson, with work by Arata Isozaki) and in proximity to the 1980s-township development of Robina in the city's south-west, Varsity Lakes began as a marriage between public and commercial interests, attracting state and municipal funding alongside commercial investment. It was, at its outset, a product of the technology bubble, built with State Government support under Queensland's Smart State rubric, seeking to exploit a booming technology economy by establishing the land around Bond University (then the city's only university) as a hub in the model of North Carolina's Research Triangle Park (visited in 1999 by then-Premier Peter Beattie and City Council delegates): the Robina Innovation Corridor.[13]

Varsity Lakes survived the millennial downturn in the technology economy through its early involvement of residential zones in an otherwise industry driven planning scheme, for which a Special Facility Zoning Plan had been adopted. In its final form, the suburb has come to serve the Australian New Urbanism movement as a model for 'good urban form', with its emphasis (following the 1994 charter *Urban Design in Australia*) on careful public space supporting community 'interaction and involvement', combining 'play, recreation, ceremony, as well as day-to-day business' in a safe and moderated environment.[14] In this sense, Varsity Lakes is both similar to and different from Helensvale. It was similar in that its conception it would function within the city on its own terms, but also advance the recently amalgamated city in a new direction, aligned with State priorities and supporting an economic foundation for the newly enlarged Gold Coast that explored opportunities beyond the

9.9 Waterfront Villa, Sanctuary Cove, Queensland (design by The Hulbert Group and Cummings and Burns), completed 1986.

tourist dollar and real estate development. Early investors had included Compaq, Boeing, and a number of telecommunications businesses, nearly all of which went elsewhere as the promise of the late 1990s fizzled.[15] While Varsity Lakes was, at its outset, torn between two competing values – expressing the technological innovation of the industries it supported and providing a model community for their employees – it has evolved as a masterplanned community, privileging the mechanisms of urban design as a form of soft governance. In this, the development's recreational facilities and mixed-use planning, schools and commercial zones offer the physical setting for a coherent community. In doing so, however, they provide a means of control that is quickly tested by shifting suburban boundaries or architectural expressions of individuality.

The Hope Island development of Sanctuary Cove – just north of Helensvale – is touted as the first masterplanned community in Australia, opened in 1986 with an event that included a live performance by Frank Sinatra. While its claim to that title is secure, it nonetheless extended the ambitions of an earlier project to design the community environments of the Gold Coast's permanent residents that had already been attempted in Helensvale itself. Varsity Lakes is curious in this setting not for the way it uses design as a mechanism of governance (defining use, scale and the relation of new works to their context), but for the extent to which it flourished after the disappearance of the industries it was conceived to support.

These suburban developments describe a version of the Gold Coast that could not be further from the tall towers on the sea edge, and which support the populations that, in turn, support the city's economy. But they also function as projects – controlled to greater or lesser degrees – that have a new kind of ambiguity in relation to the Gold Coast thanks to the intercity infrastructure established since the 1990s that has allowed the city to function, in part, as an extension of the state capital of Brisbane. By now, the traffic corridor between these two cities is the busiest in Australia, and the expanding reach of the four municipalities together defining Queensland's southeast corner has rightly earned the moniker given it by Peter Spearritt: 'the two-hundred-kilometre city'.

This is a city that is neither a beach-side paradise nor a hinterland retreat, but is comprised of the western, northern sprawl to which all east-coast Australian cities have been subject. In this, the once strictly planned communities of Helensvale and Varsity Lakes, the intentions of which having to varying degrees been diffused with time, function as models for urban-scale units of expansion. The proliferation of new subdivisions along infrastructure corridors has, wittingly or otherwise, taken these communities as their outline, shaped by such matters as investment outlooks, water and electrical services, lending practices, and traffic engineering. Like Eddie Hayes in 1958, we are left to ponder the ambiguous role left for architecture in the phenomena most directly and permanently shaping the city of the coming decades. Sixty years on from his brief but penetrating account of a much, much smaller city, architecture has traded its lot as a servant of speculative investment to take up another role (in the guise of urban design) as a tool of urban governance.

GOLD COAST

10 The City Away from it All

Milo Dunphy's frontispiece for the Gold Coast issue of *Architecture in Australia* offers a sense of a population prostrated on the beach, soaking up the heat from the sand and sun. Writing in the *Courier Mail* fifty years later, novelist Frank Moorhouse recalls: 'Maybe I saw the Gold Coast as a sort of urban nervous collapse, because as a city of holidaymakers it was a city of people exhausted from a year's work, on the edge, worn out, recovering; it understood nervous breakdowns.' It was a city that 'looked like no other Australian city' and it was a city that acted like no other. The Gold Coast, he continues, 'resembled a city that had been designed as an architect's model of a highrise city which had slipped off the table and washed up on a stretch of beautiful beach where it grew magically into real dimensions.'[1] Here, in the end, is our subject: the Gold Coast as a negotiation of ideas and reality, of intentions and their consequences, of models and their re-enactment, of image and substance.

In Matthew Condon's novel *A Night at the Pink Poodle* (1995), his protagonist Icarus – a nickname, thankfully, even if for a Gold Coast penthouse salesman – experiences his own breakdown, of sorts. In seeking to connect with something authentic, he turns to the past and to the Pink Poodle as a landmark motel on the old highway. (The motel has long-since gone, but its neon signage is protected.) He is forced to admit that as much as one can heap nostalgia upon the post-war age of innocence, the motel is no longer a destination for the family holiday so much as a place for truckers to doss, bed bugs to thrive and sex workers to ply their wares. This is no return to a golden age, but another rotation on a downward spiral. For Condon's protagonist it is a question of coping with the reconciliation of the fragile image of a better past with the realities of how the past is distorted and walled off with time: the brutal realities of development and the obsolescence it fosters among buildings and their inhabitants; the struggle to continue investing in the identity of the centre as it gives way to an anonymous sprawl; and the desire of the city itself to mature and be taken seriously, even against a backdrop of lost freedoms.[2]

What sort of city is the Gold Coast, today? While it is a city that prides itself on its distinction among Australia's urban centres, reading it alongside Henri Lefebvre's *Toward an Architecture of Enjoyment* (published in 2014, but written in 1973) prompts us to place it in a family of other cities similarly equipped to handle the nervous breakdown inherent to the urbanised, seaside retreat from the regular pace of life.[3] This new family of cities takes us away from the American references of Los Angeles, Las Vegas and Miami, and instead begins from an encounter with the Spanish resort town of Benidorm in Costa Blanca. Like the Gold Coast (and Honolulu, and Acapulco), it seemingly sprang up in the 1950s and 1960s from nowhere, sliding into

(*left*) **10.1 Gold Coast issue of**
***Architecture in Australia**, **1959**

10.2 Ying Ang, Broadbeach, 2014.

varying states of borrowed glamour and disrepute in the decades that followed. Such cities as this, argues Łukasz Stanek (who introduces the work), supply an infrastructure based on pleasure and relaxation and the paradoxical stance of offering an urbanised experience of 'getting away from' the city. The high-rises of these cities are the hotels and apartment blocks invoked by Condon and Moorhouse rather than corporate headquarters, their permanent populations oriented towards the various service industries that keep afloat an economy built on an apparently permanent transience.

Together these cities describe a threat to architecture with a capital 'A' by means of their patent subordination of architectural ideas to the logic of pleasure (and of development and real estate speculation as peculiar manifestations of the same). And a threat, too, to the maturity for which a city of substance might yearn. Again, Lefebvre: 'Unfortunately, beaches can support no constructions other than those that are forgotten. Anything more and the structure would obliterate the space of enjoyment, in the process destroying its most characteristic feature: fluidity, transition.'[4] He is wrong, of course, but these cities can never escape the sense that one serious wave can do away with it all.

The response to such criticisms as those tabled by Gruzman and Douglas (and as recalled in Chapter 8) is that outsiders simply do not *get* the Gold Coast – a singular city, as distinctive as it is divisive, replete with exceptional experiences. One forgives its ambivalent relationship with those measures to which other, older cities are beholden, by-products as they are of what architect Eddie Hayes had already described in 1958 as an enthusiastic and indiscriminate development, an era of naïve innocence and surgical cynicism to which nostalgia now accrues. It remains to history, though, to test the substance of this past, and to hold the present accountable for the values it finds therein. In this, we are left with the question of what architecture *has been* in this setting, and what, consequently, it *does* here. The postmodern moment has already done away with the distinctions we once made between high and low, origins and imitations, that would help us on our way, and there is a suite of studies from the 1970s onwards that offer some clues as to how to proceed. The Gold Coast is not Las Vegas, nor is it Los Angeles, Manhattan, or Dubai – but it does pose a conceptual problem that they all share. What is architecture's role in a city like this?

10.3 Ying Ang, Surfers Paradise, 2014.

The Gold Coast's enduring status as an historical document of Australian postmodernism still hits a raw nerve, even as postmodernism eases its way into popular fashion. In 2011, at the moment he returned to his now famed photographic survey of Surfers Paradise and its surrounds, John Gollings bemoaned the 'loss of humour and curiosity that abounded in an innocent era of homespun pleasure and unsophisticated buildings. A de-personalised affront of massed concrete is a poor replacement and an indictment of planning policies at the end of the century.' He continues: 'Recent development is more sensitive to the streetscape but nothing is as emotionally and physically accessible as the now demolished paradise!'[5]

This is not to say that the city is without notable buildings – of which there are too many left to introduce, in too few pages. Across the city are many fine houses of varying scales, and few places have had more opportunity to experiment formally with the residential high-rise than the cities along this stretch of the Pacific.[6] With the Gold Coast Cultural Precinct competition, architects from all over the world engaged with the same opportunities: OMA, Foster + Partners, Dominique Perrault, MVRDV, and so forth. Even before this, and as we have seen, the city had attracted speculative schemes by Moshe Safdie (a casino) and Zaha Hadid (a bus station), had seen realised works by architects of national and international repute, including apartments by Harry Seidler and Ian Moore – both in Broadbeach – university buildings by Arata Isozaki, Daryl Jackson and CRAB (Cook, Rowbotham Architectural Bureau), numerous buildings and, of course, the planning schemes of Karl Langer. It even boasts a riverside house designed for Kenzo Tange and his family (by an unsuspecting John Patane). The 2018 Commonwealth Games have prompted a flurry of building works including sports facilities and an athletes' village alongside the Griffith–Gold Coast University Hospital Health and Knowledge Precinct – and including, too, the extended path of the light rail system and attention to all manner of roadways and intersections that have gridlocked traffic for many months. In reciting such a roll-call, though, it is hard to ignore the feeling that the Gold Coast is a city that persists in questioning the need for architecture, as writers in *Architecture in Australia* had observed nearly sixty years ago. New projects are much more likely to be known by the name of their developer rather than their architect – and these developers have media profiles that would make any architect deeply envious.

In this, such local 'authors' as Sunland and Raptis loom large. One might still go out of one's way to cringe at the celebration of excess embodied in the Palazzo Versace (DBI Design for Sunland, 2000) or the extravagant Mediterraneanism of the Moroccan (also by DBI, opened in 1995), and one might still feel reassuringly uncomfortable while poking fun at the flurries of copy/paste in the French Quarter at Emerald Lakes (developed by Nifsan since 1991) and the Carrara replica of Michelangelo's 'David' it acquired from Raptis Plaza on Broadbeach, or its tribute to the Spanish Steps, replete with *barca*, but updated for matters of health and safety. A capacity to sustain bad taste in all its forms is, after all, the least interesting legacy of the postmodern decades.

More significantly, those decades stripped us of the illusion that architecture and culture necessarily go hand in hand, and of the illusion, too, that the intervention of the architect is a salve that can be applied to a city shaped by real estate development. While being tempted to enjoy the experience of a city revelling in its own capacity for kitsch – *Learning from Las Vegas* is the ultimate instruction manual in this respect – we still need to move beyond this layer to understand what it shares with works like Sunland's Q1 in Surfers Paradise (2006), the tallest residential tower in the southern hemisphere and one of the tallest in the world. Or indeed the qualities of the DBI-designed towers of Oracle on Broadbeach (developed by Niecon and completed in 2010). Works of the city's adolescence, they seek to outdo each other in height and capacity, with each new tower claiming the mantle of 'tallest' as the next contender for this title is yet being constructed – and all with an eye on the Council for Tall Buildings and Urban Habitat's regulations on vanity height. These works define the contemporary city image, and trade on that image in developments at all manner of scales.

10.4 Ying Ang, Behind Merrimac State
School, 2014.

The project to establish an iconic arts and culture precinct likewise traded on the city's image. Sited on the river-bend Bundall site occupied since 1971 by the Gold Coast City Council's chambers and the City Art Gallery (original buildings by Hamilton Hayes Henderson) – but which earlier on was a cotton plantation, and before that the land on which generations of Aboriginal communities lived – the project sought a middle ground between the aspirational values bound up in the city's skyline and the populism of the city's many theme parks. In an early proposal for the precinct masterplan, a proposal by Super Colossal had the city's cultural amenities marooned on an island away from the city proper, effectively mounting a criticism of the city and its historical approach to things cultural. At the same time, the competition winning scheme by a design collaboration led by the Melbourne firm of ARM Architecture – a project that has already suffered its share of compromises – invokes not only the city's penchant for spectacle, but also the forms that have solidified its commitment to leisure and hence to a very Australian sense of culture. This is, perhaps naturally, embodied in the theme parks

on the edges of the M1 at Helensvale, Ormeau and Coomera, to which the metropolitan centres remain resistant.

This sense of city management as a balancing act between the iconic gesture and its confrontation with real conditions is pursued across a series of infrastructure projects intended at one level to provide the city with the systems it requires to function at the future scale. The report *Beyond the Horizon: Imagining the Gold Coast of the Future* (2015)[7] would have the population double in the next 35 years, demanding more of the city as a machine than ever before. But even facing down a period of unprecedented population densification, it is important to recall that this rate of growth is not at all unprecedented. As the population grows and grows, the issues faced by architecture– as a profession, but also as a field of debate and experimentation – will quickly recall Hayes's frustrations over the slow provision of sewerage and poor quality of road surfaces in the face of the successive booms of the 1950s that cemented the city's place in the Australian imagination. The studies, therefore, that imagine a Gold Coast of the future all share the ambition to maintain the image locked into this time period and finessed over decades while making the process of visiting for

10.5 Ying Ang, November 14, 2:15pm,
2014.

a day, a week or a month, or investing in property, both possible and desirable. The concentration of a mass of economic activity around health and education connects literally to the city by means of a new light rail corridor that extends south from Griffith University and the hospital through Southport and Surfers Paradise down to Broadbeach, and (as of 2018) north to the 'heavy' rail line at Helensvale. While the excitement of the 1980s over the possibilities of a city-wide monorail system went the way of all such projects (realised and hoped for), the light rail network opened in 2014 and extended for 2018 has been advanced in tandem with Hassel's *Gold Coast Rapid Transit Corridor Study 2031*. It is here to stay.

This scheme for the city and its systems is typical as a project that seeks to preserve the iconic skyline, even as it manages the swathes of unrelenting sprawl that gives formless form to the Australian suburban dream. For the last half century, the Gold Coast has curated an image of itself as a scrappy upstart prepared to take risks and explore the possibilities of Australian urban life. It has built this reputation on the shoulders of its most enterprising and cynical characters, and maintained it while regularising all those matters that govern the nature and quality of the city. The amalgamation of the City of Gold Coast with Albert River Shire did more than to expand the city's territory. It also normalised the regulatory and value systems under which building and development could happen for a sprawling single-government municipality.

This is the Gold Coast's current paradox, or at least the paradox of its dense centre: a city built largely in the absence of those regulations that hold a building accountable to its neighbours, which has for the last half century sought to capture as a set of guiding principles the values of that earlier moment. And within this is its enduring challenge: to be a city capable of overcoming (to quote Pier Vittorio Aureli) 'a nostalgic reconstruction of an ideal place which has never existed.'[8]

Notes

1   To the Gold Coast

1 Robin Boyd, *The Australian Ugliness* (Melbourne: Cheshire, 1960), 31.

2 The Editors, 'Editorial I: The Challenge', special issue, *The Gold Coast*, *Architecture in Australia* 48, no. 1 (January–March 1959), n.p. Although writing anonymously, the magazine's Editorial Committee comprised of Noel Bell, Milo Dunphy (who designed the issue's gold frontispiece), Herbert Hely (partner of Bell in Hely, Bell and Horne), Morton Herman, Russell Jack, Peter Kollar (who designed the cover), Trevor Mowbray and Keith Sawdy.

3 Boyd, *The Australian Ugliness*, 91.

4 Boyd, *The Australian Ugliness*, 68–69.

5 Peter Spearritt, 'The 200 Kilometre City', in *A Climate for Growth*, ed. Brendan Gleeson and Wendy Steele (St Lucia: University of Queensland Press, 2010), 39–58.

6 For a summary of key facts and statistics, see Aysin Dedekorkut-Howes, Caryl Bosman and Andrew Leach, 'Considering the Gold Coast', in *Off the Plan: The Urbanisation of the Gold Coast*, ed. Bosman, Dedekorkut-Howes and Leach (Melbourne: CSIRO Publishing, 2015), 1–16.

7 The Editors, 'Editorial: I. The Challenge', n.p.

8 As reported in 'Architects Thumb Noses at Dozers', *Gold Coast Bulletin*, May 8, 1984.

9 Cited in Michael Jones, *A Sunny Place for Shady People: The Real Gold Coast Story* (Sydney: Allen & Unwin, 1986), 35, orig. in J. B. Priestley, *Saturn Over the Water* (London: Heinemann, 1961).

2   Under the Surface

1 This chapter draws extensively on the Local Studies Library Newspaper Clippings collection at the Southport Branch of the City of Gold Coast Libraries, specifically the files under the general subject heading 'Aborigines, Australian – Queensland – Gold Coast'. Specific articles are referenced below.

2 John Elliot, *Southport – Surfers Paradise: An Illustrated History to Commemorate the Centenary of the Southport State School* (Southport, Qld: Gold Coast and Hinterland Historical Society Museum Fund, 1980), 107.

3 Lindy Salter, *South Stradbroke Island*, 2nd ed. (South Stradbroke Island, Qld: Lindy Salter, 2002), 19.

4 The find and the story around it is documented in Laila Haglund, *An Archaeological Analysis of the Broadbeach Burial Ground* (St Lucia: University of Queensland Press, 1976).

5 'Ancient Bones to be Laid to Rest', *Gold Coast Bulletin* [*GCB*], July 30, 1985.

6 *Gold Coast Leader* [*GCL*], July 31, 1985; *GCB*, August 26, 1988 ('Skeleton in Closet Rattles Scruples'); *GCB*, August 24, 1988 ('Row over Aboriginal Remains Put to Rest').

7 'Memorial Planned for Local Family', *Kombumerri News* 4 (October 1990), 1.

8 Elliot, *Southport – Surfers Paradise*, 8.

9 'Memorial Planned for Local Family', 1.

10 See the First Australians pages at the National Museum of Australia: http://www.nma.gov.au/exhibitions/first_australians/resistance/bilin_bilin

11 Lindy Salter offers a series of clarifications over the naming of different parts of this island: 'The Aboriginal names for Stradbroke mentioned by early European observers were "Chanangarie" and "Dumba". [Several writers] called the south island "Minjerriba" as this was the name used by the local people for the southern end of the island and the adjacent mainland. However, later writers … have popularised its use for North Stradbroke. The word is close to "Moondarewa", thought to have derived from an Aboriginal word meaning "mosquito". Hanlon wrote that the Aboriginal name, "Moonjeribah" (or Welsby's "Moondaraba") was changed to "Moondarewa" by the

surveyor who mapped the southern end of Stradbroke for land sales.' She notes the current name of 'Gurrangul' for South Stradbroke Island. Salter, *South Stradbroke Island*, 19. This level of historical uncertainty around the transliteration of oral names into written form persists across the whole region, if not the continent entire.

12 Salter, *South Stradbroke Island*, 18.

13 Tim O'Rourke, 'Aboriginal Camps and "Villages" in Southeast Queensland', in *Open*, ed. Alexandra Brown and Andrew Leach, *Proceedings of the Society of Architectural Historians, Australia and New Zealand* 30 (Southport, Qld: SAHANZ, 2013), vol. 2, 851.

14 O'Rourke, 'Aboriginal Camps and "Villages" in Southeast Queensland', 858.

15 O'Rourke, 'Aboriginal Camps and "Villages" in Southeast Queensland', 852–854.

16 O'Rourke, 'Aboriginal Camps and "Villages" in Southeast Queensland', 860–61.

17 O'Rourke, 'Aboriginal Camps and "Villages" in Southeast Queensland', 856. Quoting from James Backhouse, *A Narrative of a Visit to the Australian Colonies* (London: Hamilton Adams, 1843).

18 'Aborigines left with memories', *Gold Coast Sun* [*GCS*], October 26, 2005.

19 'Aboriginal Stone Relics are Saved Just in Time', *GCB* February 19, 1986.

20 'Disturbance of Midden Unfortunate, Says Pie', *GCB*, January 18, 1986.

21 'Preserving History', *GCB*, January 11, 1986.

22 'Car Park Planned for Aboriginal Midden', *GCB*, November 17, 1995.

23 Robert Longhurst, 'The Gold Coast: Its First Inhabitants', *John Oxley Journal* 1, no. 2 (1980), 22–24.

24 Ysola Best in Johanna Kijas, *Everyone knew Everyone: A Community History of Burleigh Heads* (Bundall, Qld: Gold Coast City Council, 2008), 19.

25 'The First Tourists', *GCB*, December 15, 1995; 'Aborigines Love Coast Holidays Too', *GCS*, January 29, 1997. Both articles refer to Frank Hampson, *In the Beginning was the Dreamtime: Paradise Dreaming: The History and the Spirit of the Gold Coast* (Surfers Paradise, Qld: Gold Coast City Council, 1995).

26 'Links with Aboriginal Past May be Listed', *GCB*, January 7, 1986.

27 Robert Longhurst, *The Heart of Paradise: The History of Burleigh Heads* (Surfers Paradise, Qld: Gold Coast City Council, 1991), 9.

28 Longhurst, 'The Gold Coast', 21.

3 River Bound

1 Reyner Banham, *Los Angeles: The Architecture of Four Ecologies* (1971; London: Pelican, 1973), 24–25.

2 'The Northern Settlements: Moreton Bay', *Sydney Colonist*, December 24, 1835.

3 Hector Holthouse, *Illustrated History of the Gold Coast* (Frenchs Forest, NSW: Reed, 1982), 5.

4 Michael Jones, *A Sunny Place for Shady People: The Real Gold Coast Story* (Sydney: Allen & Unwin, 1986), 15.

5 Michael Jones, *Country of Five Rivers: Albert Shire, 1788–1988* (Sydney: Allen & Unwin, 1988), 55.

6 Jones, *Country of Five Rivers*, 57, 58.

7 Jones, *A Sunny Place for Shady People*, 15.

8 Holthouse, *Illustrated History of the Gold Coast*, 15.

9 Jones, *A Sunny Place for Shady People*, 15.

10 Jones, *Country of Five Rivers*, 1.

11 Jones, *Country of Five Rivers*, 50.

12 John Elliott (ed.) *Letters to Bundall 1872–1879 and Lena Cooper's Manuscript* (Southport, Qld: Gold Coast & Hinterland Historical Society, 1993), 277.

13 Jones, *Country of Five Rivers*, 1.

14 In Elliott (ed.), *Letters to Bundall*, 268, see also www.goldcoaststories.com.au.

15 Holthouse, *Illustrated History of the Gold Coast*, 13.

16 Holthouse, *Illustrated History of the Gold Coast*, 18, 20.

17 Jones, *Country of Five Rivers*, 179–81.

18 Jones, *Country of Five Rivers*, 67.

4 On the Beach

1 'The Southport Railway: The Opening Ceremony', *Brisbane Courier*, January 25, 1889.

2 T. P. S., 'A Trip to Southport and Burleigh Heads', *Brisbane Courier*, March 12, 1883.

3 T. P. S., 'A Trip to Southport and Burleigh Heads'.

4 T. P. S., 'A Trip to Southport and Burleigh Heads'. See also Robert Longhurst, *The Heart of Paradise: The History of Burleigh Heads* (Surfers Paradise, Qld: Gold Coast City Council, 1991).

5 For a brief summary, see Hector Holthouse, *Illustrated History of the Gold Coast* (Frenchs Forest, NSW: Reed, 1982), ch. 10, 'The Crowds Arrive', 36–41.

6 *Coolangatta: Point of Difference*, brochure (Southport, Qld: Heritage Advisory Service and Local Studies Library, 2000).

7 Holthouse, *Illustrated History of the Gold Coast*, 25.

8 Holthouse, *Illustrated History of the Gold Coast*, 42.

9 Peter Spearritt, 'Bodies on the Gold Coast', in Graham Burstow, *Flesh: The Gold Coast in the 60s, 70s and 80s* (St Lucia: University of Queensland Press, 2014), 10.

10 Spearritt in *Flesh*, 76.

5 Gold on the Sand

1 E. J. W. (Edward James A. Weller), 'Queensland', *Architecture in Australia* [*AA*] 47, no. 1 (January–March 1958), 72–73.

2 Morton Herman, 'Recent Governmental Architecture in Queensland', 74–76; Neville H. Lund, 'Robin S. Dods: The Life and Work of a Distinguished Queensland

Architect', 77–86; and E. J. Hayes, 'Gold on the Sand', 87; all in *AA* 47, no. 1 (January–March 1958). All quotations from Hayes's article in these pages are from this single source.

3 Aysin Dedekorkut-Howes, Caryl Bosman and Andrew Leach, 'Considering the Gold Coast,' *Off the Plan: The Urbanisation of the Gold Coast*, ed. Bosman, Dedekorkut-Howes and Leach (Melbourne: CSIRO Publishing, 2016), 4–8.

4 See Aysin Dedekorkut-Howes and Severine Mayere, 'City with/out a Plan', in *Off the Plan*, 138–139.

5 Alexander McRobbie, for instance, makes mention of a 'Chinese syndicate' financing a serviced apartment building in 1952. McRobbie, *The Gold Coast Story* (Surfers Paradise: The Gold Coast Annual Company, 1966), 23.

6 Michael Jones, *A Sunny Place for Shady People: The Real Gold Coast Story* (Sydney: Allen & Unwin, 1986), 22.

7 Andrew Wilson and Angela Reilly, 'Reflections on an Enduring Partnership', in *Hayes & Scott: Post-war Houses*, ed. Andrew Wilson (St Lucia: University of Queensland Press, 2005), 14–15. For a catalogue of projects, see 16–33. See, too, Andrew Wilson, 'The Houses of Hayes and Scott (1946–1984)', PhD diss., University of Queensland, 2015.

8 Alice Hampson, 'Eddie Hayes: Two Houses Built for Women', in *Hayes & Scott*, 63–68.

9 J. B. Chifley, foreword to 'The Architecture of Australia', special issue, *Architectural Review* 104, no. 619 (July 1948). Langer's project was published in the dossier 'Modern Architecture in Australia: A Pictorial Overview', 20–39.

10 On Korman, see Jones, *A Sunny Place for Shady People*, 24–28.

11 On Lennon's and heritage challenges it raises, see Alexandra Teague, 'Materialising the Immaterial: Social Value and the Conservation of Recent Everyday Places', PhD diss., University of Melbourne, 2004, ch. 7.

12 Katherine Rickard, 'Run to Paradise: The Chevron Hotel, Gold Coast, from Foundation to Renaissance', in *Open*, ed. Alexandra Brown and Andrew Leach, *Proceedings of the Society of Architectural Historians, Australia and New Zealand* 30 (Southport, Qld: SAHANZ, 2013), 58.

13 Karl Langer, 'A Hotel of a Special Kind', *Architecture, Building, Structural Engineering* 34, no. 12 (December 1956), 3.

14 Jones, *A Sunny Place for Shady People*, 26–27; Rickard, 'Run to Paradise', 63–64.

15 Karl Langer, 'Development of Canal Estate on the Gold Coast', *AA* 48, no. 1 (January–March 1959), 64.

16 On this and other distinct developments on the Gold Coast, see the University of Queensland project 'Queensland Places', online at www.queenslandplaces.com.au (in this case, under 'Broadbeach Waters').

17 Ian Sinnamon, 'An Educated Eye: Karl Langer in Australia', *Landscape Architecture* 7, no. 1 (February 1985): 48–56; cited in Robert Freestone, *Urban Nation: Australia's Planning Heritage* (Melbourne: CSIRO Publishing, 2010), 194.

18 *The Paradise City Story* (brochure) (Surfers Paradise, Qld: Bruce Small Enterprises, 1959).

19 Jones, *A Sunny Place for Shady People*, 32.

6 City of Types

1 The Editors, 'Editorial II: The Region', *Architecture in Australia* 48, no. 1 (January–March 1959) [*AA* (1959)], n.p.

2 H. J. Hitch, 'The Spa and Sea Resort', *AA* (1959), 51. His italics.

3 Hitch, 'The Spa and Sea Resort', 52.

4 Peter Newell, 'Umbigumbi to the Gold Coast', *AA* (1959), 73.

5 Newell, 'Umbigumbi to the Gold Coast', 73.

6 Milo Dunphy, 'An Ideal Holiday Resort on the Gold Coast', *AA* (1959), 53.

7 László Peter Kollar, 'The Gold Coast and the Principles of Regional Development', *AA* (1959), 58.

8 Kollar, 'The Gold Coast', 63.

9 Karl Langer, 'Development of Canal Estate on the Gold Coast', *AA* (1959), 64–65.

10 The Editors, 'Editorial 3: The Estates', *AA* (1959), n.p.

11 Marjorie St Henry, 'The Town Council's Obligations on The Gold Coast'; J. H. Shaw, 'Can We Have Paradise Without Suburbia?'; C. A. Kelly, 'NSW North Has Outstanding Holiday Future', *AA* (1959), 82, 83 and 84, resp.

12 Robin Boyd, *The Australian Ugliness* (Melbourne, Vic.: Cheshire, 1960), 69.

13 The Editors, 'Editorial I: The Challenge', *AA* (1959), n.p.

14 The Editors, 'Editorial 4: The Architecture', *AA* (1959), n.p.

15 'Institute News', *AA* (1959), 85.

16 Michael Jones, *A Sunny Place for Shady People* (Sydney: Allen & Unwin, 1986), 38.

17 Jones, *A Sunny Place for Shady People*, 79.

18 *Living High: An Architectural Guide to Tall Buildings on the Gold Coast* (Southport, Qld: Gold Coast Heritage Advisory Service, 1997).

19 Jones, *A Sunny Place for Shady People*, 129, 135.

20 Allom Lovell Marquis Kyle, Henchall Hanson & Associates, et al., *Gold Coast Urban Heritage & Character Study* (Surfers Paradise, Qld: Gold Coast City Council, 1997).

21 Philip Goad, 'The Gold Coast: Architecture and Planning', *Gold Coast Urban Heritage & Character Study*, 37–41, esp. 38–39, 41.

7 Vegas in Paradise

1 Robert Venturi, Denise Scott Brown and Steven Izenour, *Learning from Las Vegas* (Cambridge, Mass.: MIT Press, 1972). It is widely known but worth reiterating here that *Learning from Las Vegas* (revised and reformatted in 1977) recorded the research and thinking of students from the Yale School of Art and Architecture in a travelling research studio lead by Robert Venturi, Denise Scott Brown and Steven Izenour in 1968. On which, see Hilar Stadler and Martino Stierli, eds, *Las Vegas Studio: Images from the Archives of Robert Venturi and Denise Scott Brown* (Zurich: Scheidegger & Spiess, 2008).

2 Pers. comm. Gordon Holden to Andrew Leach, May 12, 2015; and Styant-Browne to Leach, August 28, 2014 and May 30, 2015.

3 On Corbett Lyon on this studio at Penn, see 'Learning from the Venturis', dir. Toby Reed and Sam Reed (Nervegna Reed Architects and RMIT Design Hub), online at https://www.youtube.com; also, Steven Izenour, Mark Hewitt, Paul Muller, Corbett Lyon, George E. Thomas and Julie Heller, *Atlantic City Historic Buildings Survey* (Atlantic City, NJ: Office of Historic Preservation, 1980).

4 Virginia Rigney, 'Motion View: The Car and the City', in John Gollings, *Learning from Surfers Paradise* (Surfers Paradise, Qld: Gold Coast City Gallery, 2013), 61–62.

5 John Gollings, 'Fixing Time: Making a Rephotography Project', in *Learning from Surfers Paradise*, 5.

6 Tony Styant-Browne, 'Knowledge Needs for Quality Design', in *The Knowledge Needs for Architectural Practice: Knowing How to Know*, ed. Susan Savage (Brisbane: Queensland University of Technology, 1995), 40.

7 The date range refers to 1973 as the year in which the original project was planned, and 2013 to the year in which the new photographs (taken 2008–12) were first exhibited. All image pairs in the catalogue are dated 1973/2013, as are the photographic pairs reproduced here.

8 *Las Vegas Studio/Learning from Surfers Paradise* was staged on the Gold Coast to coincide with the thirtieth annual conference of the Society of Architectural Historians, Australia and New Zealand (Griffith University, July 2–5, 2013) and was an initiative of the Gold Coast City Gallery.

9 Kevin A. Lynch, *Image of the City* (Cambridge, Mass.: MIT Press 1960); Gordon Cullen, *Townscape* (London: Architectural Press, 1961).

8 A Profession Organised

1 Jeff Licence (dir.), *Drawn Here* (Tiger Monkey, 2013, online at youtube.com). Unless otherwise mentioned, all quotations from architects in this chapter are from the interviews in this short documentary film.

2 This chapter draws extensively on the ephemera, newspaper cutting file and press release records of the Gold Coast and Northern Rivers Region of the RAIA, hereafter called the Gold Coast Architecture Awards Archive (GCAAA).

3 This chapter is excerpted from the introduction to Andrew Leach, Katherine Rickard and Finn Jones, *GC30+: Documenting the Gold Coast Architecture Awards* (Southport, Qld: Griffith University Urban Research Program, 1984–2013), online at issuu.com/leachas. For further details on the chairs of the Division, see p. 8 of that document.

4 Bill Heather, 'Sunshine and Sensuality', ms of talk to *Insite/Outsight*, RAIA Queensland Chapter Convention, Brisbane, 1978 (Gold Coast Architecture Awards Archives), n.p.

5 Bill Heather, 'Sunshine and Sensuality', n.p.

6 For details on each year's juries and decisions, see *GC30+*, 10, and the dossiers commencing on p. 18.

7 Murray Simpson, 'Search on Again for the Best Building Designs', *Gold Coast Bulletin* [*GCB*], April 27, 1985; Tim Bailey, 'Modest Building Wins Main Award, High Rises Fail to Impress Judges', *GCB*, May 11, 1985 (GCAAA).

8 Quoted in Michael Jones, *A Sunny Place for Shady People: The Real Gold Coast Story* (Sydney: Allen & Unwin, 1986), 48–49.

9 RAIA media releases, April 24, May 8, 16, 1986 (GCAAA).

10 RAIA media releases April 28, May 5, 7, 1987 (GCAAA).

11 RAIA media releases, May 9, 13, 19, 1988 (GCAAA).

12 RAIA media releases, May 15, 18, 26, 1989 (GCAAA).

13 RAIA media releases, May 10, 21, 30, 31, 1991 (GCAAA).

14 RAIA media releases, May 16, 19, 1994 (GCAAA).

15 RAIA Gold Coast Architecture Awards Overview, May 28, 1999 (GCAAA).

16 RAIA Gold Coast Architecture Awards Overview, May 28, 1999 (GCAAA).

17 Hannah Sbeghen, 'Couran Cove Offering Permanent Low Rentals While Undergoing Makeover', *GCB*, July 19, 2017.

18 Gordon Holden, 'What, if Anything, Can be Made of the Gold Coast Urban Design Awards?', in *Open*, ed. Alexandra Brown and Andrew Leach, *Proceedings of the Society of Architectural Historians, Australian and New Zealand* 30 (Southport, Qld: SAHANZ 2013), vol. 1, 389–406. Compare, too, the discussion on urban design in Pier Vittorio Aureli, *The Possibility of an Absolute Architecture* (Cambridge, Mass.: MIT Press, 2011), 1–47.

9 Community Planning

1 H. E. Michael Bryce, speech to the Gold Coast and Northern Rivers Region of the Australian Institute of Architects, Palazzo Versace, April 20, 2013, ms.

2 Michael Jones, *A Sunny Place for Shady People: The Real Gold Coast Story* (Sydney: Allen & Unwin, 1986), 3, 6.

3 'Helensvale Sold; Was to have been Community Settlement', *South Coast Bulletin*, March 8, 1950. All articles referenced in this chapter are collected in Local Studies Library Newspaper Clippings files at the Southport Branch of the City of Gold Coast Libraries, under 'Helensvale'.

4 As reported in the *Gold Coast Bulletin* [*GCB*], February 21, 1976.

5 As reported in the *GCB*, February 9, 1978.

6 'Estate Takes 500th Family', *Courier Mail*, October 2, 1982.

7 'Helensvale Celebrates 10th Year and Successful Planning', *Hinterlander*, April 18, 1984.

8 'Helensvale – top of a housing iceberg', *Courier Mail*, February 8, 1982.

9 'A Man with Designs on Better Ways of Living', *GCB*, December 4, 1980.

10 'A Man with Designs on Better Ways of Living', *GCB*.

11 *World of Helensvale* 8, no. 2 (April 1986), 1.

12 'Helensvale at Final Few Stages', *GCB*, July 31–August 1, 1993.

13 Marit Askbo, 'Something Old, Something New, Something Borrowed, Something Blue: The Case of Varsity Lakes', hons. diss. (Urban and Environmental Planning), Griffith University, 2012, 2, 37.

14 The Urban Design Taskforce, quoted in Askbo, 'Something Old, Something New', 31.

15 Askbo, 'Something Old, Something New', 44.

10 The City Away from it All

1 Frank Moorhouse, 'Pleasure Dome in Paradise', *Courier Mail*, December 17, 2011.

2 Matthew Condon, *A Night at the Pink Poodle* (North Sydney, NSW: Vintage, 1995).

3 Henri Lefebvre, *Toward an Architecture of Enjoyment*, ed. Łukasz Stanek (Minneapolis: University of Minnesota Press, 2014), 3.

4 Lefebvre, *Toward an Architecture of Enjoyment*, 49.

5 John Gollings, *Then and Now: The Surfers Paradise Rephotography Project 1973–2011*, exh. cat. (Bundall, Qld: Gold Coast City Gallery, 2011), n.p.

6 On which, see *GC30+: Documenting the Gold Coast Architecture Awards, 1984–2013* (Southport, Qld: Griffith University Urban Studies Program, 2015), available online (see Further Reading).

7 Published at www.futuregoldcoast.com.

8 Pier Vittorio Aureli, *The Possibility of an Absolute Architecture* (Cambridge, Mass.: MIT Press, 2011), 32.

Further Reading

Addington, Brett, Mandana Mapar and Virginia Rigney (cur.). *All that Glitters: Contemporary Visions of the Gold Coast*, exh. cat. Surfers Paradise, Qld: Gold Coast City Art Gallery, 2004.

Allom Lovell Marquis-Kyle, Henshall Hansen, Context, HJM and Staddon Consulting. *Gold Coast Urban Heritage and Character Study*. Surfers Paradise, Qld: Gold Coast City Council, 1997.

Ang, Ying. *Gold Coast*. Melbourne: Ying Ang, 2014.

Backhouse, James. *A Narrative of a Visit to the Australian Colonies*, chap. 33. London: Hamilton, Adams and Co., 1843.

Best, Ysola and Alex Barlow. *Kombumerri, Saltwater People*. Port Melbourne, Vic.: Heinemann, 1997.

Bosman, Caryl, Aysin Dedekorkut-Howes and Andrew Leach (eds). *Off the Plan: The Urbanisation of the Gold Coast*. Melbourne: CSIRO Publishing, 2016.

Boyd, Robin. *The Australian Ugliness*. Melbourne: Cheshire, 1960.

Burstow, Graham. *Flesh: The Gold Coast in the 60s, 70s and 80s*. St Lucia: University of Queensland Press, 2014.

Burton, Paul. 'Growing Pains: Adolescent Urbanism on the Gold Coast'. *Geodate* 25, no. 2 (2012): 8–11.

Coghill, Gloria. *125 Years of Schooling on the Commera, 1873–1998*. Wongawallen, Qld: Gloria A. Coghill, 1998.

Davis, Mike and Daniel Bertrand Monk (eds). *Evil Paradises: Dreamworlds of Neoliberalism*. New York: New Press, 2007.

Elliott, John (ed.). *Letters to Bundall 1872–1879 and Lena Cooper's Manuscript*. Southport, Qld: Gold Coast and Hinterland Historical Society, 1993.

Elliot, John. *Southport—Surfers Paradise: An Illustrated History to Commemorate the Centenary of the Southport State School*. Southport, Qld: Gold Coast and Hinterland Historical Society Museum Fund, 1980.

Fitzgerald, Ross. *A History of Queensland from 1915 to the 1980s*. St Lucia: University of Queensland Press, 1984.

Freestone, Robert. *Urban Nation: Australia's Planning Heritage*. Melbourne: CSIRO Publishing, 2010.

Gollings, John. *Learning from Surfers Paradise*. Surfers Paradise, Qld: Arts Centre Gold Coast, 2013.

Gray, Phil. *A History of the World of Helensvale*. Helensvale, Qld: Helensvale Residents' Association, 2010.

Hagland, Laila. *An Archaeological Analysis of the Broadbeach Aboriginal Burial Ground*. St Lucia: University of Queensland Press, 1976.

Hajdu, Joseph. *Samurai in the Surf: The Arrival of the Japanese on the Gold Coast in the 1980s*. Canberra: Pandanus, 2005.

Hall, Jay. 'Sitting on the Crop of the Bay: An Historical and Archaeological Sketch of Aboriginal Settlement and Subsistence in Moreton Bay, Southeast Queensland'. In *Coastal Archaeology in Eastern Australia: Proceedings of the 1980 Valla Conference on Australian Prehistory*, ed. Sandra Bowdler, 79–95. Canberra, ACT: Department of Prehistory, Australian National University.

Hampson, Frank. *In the Beginning was the Dreamtime: Paradise Dreaming: The History and the Spirit of the Gold Coast*. Surfers Paradise, Qld: Gold Coast City Council, 1995.

Holthouse, Hector. *Illustrated History of the Gold Coast*. Frenchs Forrest, NSW: Reed, 1982.

Jones, Michael. *Country of Five Rivers: Albert Shire, 1788–1988*. Sydney: Allen & Unwin, 1988.

Jones, Michael. *A Sunny Place for Shady People: The Real Gold Coast Story*. Sydney: Allen & Unwin, 1986.

Kijas, Johanna. *Everyone knew Everyone: A Community History of Burleigh Heads*. Bundall, Qld: Gold Coast City Council, 2008.

Leach, Andrew, Katherine Rickard and Finn Jones. *GC30+: Documenting the Gold Coast Architecture Awards,*

1984–2013. Southport, Qld: Griffith University Urban Research Program, 2015. Online at www.issuu.com/leachas.

Longhurst, Robert. 'The Gold Coast: Its First Inhabitants', *John Oxley Journal* 1, no. 2 (1980): 15–24.

Longhurst, Robert. *Nerang Shire: A History to 1949*. Nerang, Qld: Albert Shire Council, 1994.

Longhurst, Robert. *The Heart of Paradise: The History of Burleigh Heads*. Surfers Paradise, Qld: Gold Coast City Council, 1991.

McRobbie, Alexander. *20th Century Gold Coast People*. Surfers Paradise, Qld: Gold Coast Arts Centre, 2000.

McRobbie, Alexander. *The Real Surfers Paradise from Seaside Village to International Resort*. Surfers Paradise, Qld: Pan News, 1988.

McRobbie, Alexander. *The Fabulous Gold Coast*. Surfers Paradise, Qld: Pan News, 1984.

McRobbie, Alexander. *The Surfers Paradise Story*. Surfers Paradise, Qld: Pan News, 1982.

McRobbie, Alexander (ed.). *The Gold Coast Story*. Surfers Paradise, Qld: Gold Coast Annual Co., 1966.

Newell, Peter and Kevin Jopson. *Gold Coast and Green Mountains Sketchbook*. Kent Town, SA: Rigby, 1969.

O'Connor, Rory. *The Kombumerri: Aboriginal People of the Gold Coast*. Brisbane, 1997.

O'Rourke, Tim. 'Aboriginal Camps and "Villages" in Southeast Queensland', in *Open*, ed. Alexandra Brown and Andrew Leach, *Proceedings of the Society of Architectural Historians, Australia and New Zealand* 30, vol. 2, 851–863. Southport, Qld: SAHANZ, 2013.

Paradise City, special issue, *Surf, Sun and Sand* 3, no. 2 (Winter 1960).

Remembering Our Ancestors, brochure. Southport, Qld: Keeaira Press, n.d.

Rix, Dawn Hasemann. *Labrador: The Early Pioneers*. Main Beach, Qld: DHR Publishing, 2002.

Salter, Lindy. *South Stradbroke Island*, 2nd ed. South Stadbroke Island, Qld: Lindy Salter, 2002.

Small, Bruce and Mike Nicholas. *Gold Coast Sketchbook*. Kent Town, SA: Rigby, 1981.

Steele, John. *Explorers of the Moreton Bay District 1770–1830*. St Lucia: University of Queensland Press, 1972.

Teague, Alexandra. 'Materialising the Immaterial: Social Value and the Conservation of Recent Everyday Places'. PhD diss., University of Melbourne, 2004.

Wilson, Andrew. 'The Houses of Hayes & Scott (1946–1984)'. PhD diss., University of Queensland, 2015.

Wilson, Andrew (ed.). *Hayes & Scott: Post-war Houses*. St Lucia: University of Queensland Press, 2005.

Wise, Pat. 'Australia's Gold Coast: A City Reproducing Itself'. In *Urban Space and Cityscapes: Perspectives from Modern and Contemporary Culture*, ed. Christoph Lindner, 177–191. London: Routledge, 2006.

See, too, the following websites:
www.goldcoaststories.com.au
www.queenslandplaces.com.au
www.qhatlas.com.au

Newspaper articles and ephemera referenced throughout draws principally on the clippings files of the Gold Coast Libraries Local Studies Collection, Southport, Queensland.

Index

Note: page numbers in *italics* are for illustrations

Illustration Credits

The reproduction of the illustrations listed below is courtesy of the following copyright holders: